REVISED AND UPDATED

LIVE

DEBT-

FREE

How to Quickly Pay Off Your
Credit Cards, Personal Loans, and
Mortgages—and Build Real Wealth Today!

Ted Carroll

ADAMS MEDIA
AVON, MASSACHUSETTS

Published by
Adams Media, an F+W Publications Company
57 Littlefield Street, Avon, MA 02322
www.adamsmedia.com

ISBN: 1-58062-942-3

Printed in the United States of America.

J I H G F E D C B A

Library of Congress Cataloging-in Publications Data
Carroll, Ted, 1925–1998
Live debt-free / Ted Carroll.-- 2nd ed.
p.   cm.
ISBN 1-58062-942-3
1. Finance, Personal. 2. Debt. I. Title.
HG179.C335 2003
332.024'02--dc21
2003006181

This publication is designed to provide accurate and authoritative information
with regard to the subject matter covered. It is sold with the understanding that
the publisher is not engaged in rendering legal, accounting, or other professional
advice. If legal advice or other expert assistance is required, the services of a
competent professional person should be sought.
—From a *Declaration of Principles* jointly adopted by a Committee of the
American Bar Association and a Committee of Publishers and Associations

Many of the designations used by manufacturers and sellers to distinguish their
products are claimed as trademarks. Where those designations appear in this
book and Adams Media was aware of a trademark claim, the designations have
been printed with initial capital letters.

This book is available at quantity discounts for bulk purchases.
For information, call 1-800-872-5627.

Dedication

To Virginia . . .
who lived this book before I wrote it.

A few years out of college, before she was married, she bought
her first house and paid the mortgage within five years.

Her system works. It worked for her. It works well for us. It can
work for you, too.

*In loving memory of Ted Carroll, a true original,
who brought the* Live Debt-Free *concept to life.*

Acknowledgments

Special thanks to the team at Adams Media: Tracy Quinn McLennan and Courtney Nolan, who worked with me every step of the way during reprint; Kate McBride, Laura MacLaughlin, and Lesley Bolton.

—Virginia Carroll

Contents

Preface

To the reader . . .

Chapter Three, showing you how to own your own home mortgage-free in only 10 years, is the logical first step in living debt-free. Once you're paying yourself, instead of the bank, that big chunk of money each month, other budget categories quickly fall in line.

The mortgage figures cited, 5% to 15%, are merely examples. Rates fluctuate; in a recent span of two decades they have ranged from 20% in some areas to a low of 5%.

But regardless of current rates as you read this, the principle remains the same. By following (as explained) the two steps to mortgage-free living:

(a) If rates are high, *you save even more* than in the examples.
(b) If rates are low, *you pay even less* overall.

Either way, it works. Try it.
You'll be glad you did.
. . . From the writer

Introduction

There is only one rule I would ask you to follow in reading this book: Keep an open mind.

Some of the techniques discussed here will seem a little adventurous. That's because they are. However, I would draw a distinction between "adventurous" and "dangerous." If followed prudently—and, where appropriate, with the advice of a financial counselor—the ideas presented in these pages are much less "dangerous" than the status quo.

And what is the status quo? Put simply, it is to *make it easy for the bank or whoever is handling the financing to make money.* When we sign a mortgage, buy a car on time, or order something on television with a credit card, we are usually ceding a good hunk of income for . . . what? Convenience? Tradition?

I think if you look without prejudice at the ideas contained in this book, you will find that, when it comes to your money, the traditional way of doing things—specifically, the way houses are usually bought—is just too expensive. As for convenience, you might come away from these pages with a new idea of how much you're willing to pay for it.

Good luck!

—Ted Carroll, 1991

Welcome to the updated, expanded *Live Debt-Free*.

Do you want to be a debt-ridden slave to the finance company, bank, or mortgage company?

Or would you rather live a happy, debt-free life doing things you enjoy because the money's in *your* pocket, not *theirs?*

I'm convinced that because you're holding the updated, expanded version of *Live Debt-Free* in your hand, you want to keep your money there, too.

You'll find that you can do it easily.

And, if you have trouble with math and numbers, don't worry. So do I. *Live Debt-Free* isn't about math, or even money.

It's about life—debt-free and fun.

And people.

You'll meet the Happy Spenders: Hap Spendy, Sis, Junior, Floppy the dog, and Petunia the cat; Al and Alice Interestpayer; Sam and Sue Sharp; Owen Owing; Luckless Luke and Knowledgeable Kevin; Susie Q. Smarts; and Tim and Tanya Takecharge.

Watch them make decisions that will affect the rest of their lives as they buy and build houses, shop for cars, create budgets, or plan their retirement.

Which ones will follow the *Live Debt-Free* plan?

Will they manage their money or will their money manage them?

How happy will the Happy Spenders be when the bills come in?

What will they do about it?

Will they have a happy, debt-free ending?

Will you?

The idea for *Live Debt-Free* began when my husband, Ted, who loved math, and I, who hated it, agreed on two things: (1) Staying out of debt is the only way to live happily; and (2) You don't have to worry about math to do it.

For Ted, math was always a snap.

After his third-grade class had finished multiplication, it was time for division.

When the teacher asked the class what that meant, Ted answered: "Simple. Just reverse the process!"

Although Ted excelled at math, writing would be his calling. He was a genius at both.

Ted's newspaper career encompassed every aspect of the business, from editing his elementary school paper through various reporting and writing posts in five states. Then, at 33, he won his first newspaper editor's position over hundreds of other candidates.

He became a prize-winning newspaper editor, noted for a light touch on heavy topics, especially economics. His editorials were widely reprinted in major newspapers, including the *Christian Science Monitor*, in magazines, and in diverse publications ranging from the newsletters of Wall Street brokerage firms to a plumbers' union house organ.

They were condensed in the *Conservative Digest, Reader's Digest*, and others. His commentary on the economic scene spanned 23 years as editor of the Bradenton, Florida *Herald*; editorial page editor of the Delaware County, Pennsylvania *Daily Times*; and in Jacksonville, Florida, as the associate editor, editorial page for *The Florida Times-Union*.

Besides nonfiction, Ted wrote internationally published fiction, including a novel, *White Pills* (Crown), and 144 short stories appearing in 20 magazines, newspapers, postcards and newsletters, two anthologies, and a tape recording.

Knights in Shining Tow Trucks is a collection of almost half of the 109 short stories that appeared for a decade (from April 1988 until November 1998) in virtually every monthly issue of

Tow Times®, a trade magazine that offers safety tips, legal help, and other assistance for towing and recovery professionals. The series of stories chronicled the adventures of the characters of Gus, a tow truck owner, and his wife, Mae.

Ted could write anything.

But he despised spelling.

When his father tried to persuade him to study it, he balked.

Once he asked Ted, "What will you do when you grow up? What about business reports?"

"Oh," six-year-old Ted shot back, "I'll have a secretary for that!"

His idea was: "Why worry? Write it the way it sounds."

He used his inimitable spelling throughout his writing career.

For me, spelling wasn't a problem.

Math was.

My career wasn't D for "distinguished." It was D for "difficult"—seven Ds and an F between third grade and college—and sometimes I felt D for "dumb." While numbers, x's, and y's, threw me, $$$s didn't.

And, fortunately, the year before my first D, I learned a crucial life lesson: how to avoid another D—"debt."

It was May 16, 1956. The sun shone brightly as I happily hopscotched home from second grade.

School was almost out. Swimming, hide-and-seek, and playing danced in my mind as I bounced up the front steps two by two.

I threw open the door.

Then stopped.

Although I couldn't understand all the ramifications just then, I sensed that more than summer vacation was afoot.

Things *felt* different.

Before I knew it, my whole family was in the basement, in front of the fireplace where a crackling fire glowed. Hors d'oeuvres and ginger ale adorned a table nearby.

What's going on? I wondered. Why is there a fire in May?

I glanced at my father as he vertically ripped a piece of paper. With a flourish, he handed a portion to each of us.

I heard "mort"-something and "now the house is ours."

Hasn't it always been? I've been here all my life, I thought.

All seven of us had a slice of the "mort"-something to throw into the fire.

First my father.

Then my mother.

Then the children: TAVRE (Tom, Anne, Virginia, Roger, and Elizabeth) in turn, by ages.

Tossing my slice into the fire, I didn't know that the celebration was the first of three $20,000 payoffs I'd enjoy.

But I knew one thing: We owed no one. The house was truly *ours*.

As we toasted with the ginger ale and munched the hors d'oeuvres, I made up my mind: I didn't want to owe anyone either. And I was going to pay off my house when I grew up, too.

My second-grade self declared: "I'm going to live debt-free!"

The vow would be reinforced the next fall when my third-grade teacher explained credit and loan interest.

Although I'd gotten a D in math, I understood the value of living debt-free.

"Interest?" I asked. "Why do they call it 'interest'? I'm not *interested* in it. Who wants to pay more than you owe?"

Then "credit" came up, and a similar question arose in my third-grade mind.

Each day, the teacher took orders for cartons of milk, white or chocolate, for whoever wanted one. Collecting "milk money," she asked, "Do you want to pay now or get it on credit?"

"Credit?" I asked. "Why does someone get credit for not paying for the milk now?"

We'd paid off our *house*. Couldn't they pay cash for a carton of *milk*?

I promised myself anew: no "credit" or "interest" for me.

Fifteen years after the interest/credit/debt burning bush glowed in my family's fireplace during the mortgage burning, I would encounter my initial debt-free challenge.

Time for my first car.

Although tired of standing in the cold and heat to catch the bus to John Knox Press in Richmond, Virginia (now Westminster John Knox Press in Louisville, Kentucky), where I worked, I remembered my promise.

No debt. Thus, no car loans.

I wasn't "interested" in throwing away money on interest for years.

Cash it was.

I'd wait.

In a year I'd finally saved enough to drive a new, free-and-clear car out of the showroom.

Then, in 1972, debt-free and weary of cold weather, I drove my paid-for car to Jacksonville, Florida, to work with three other editors at *The Florida Times-Union*.

Ted was one.

We kidded him about his creative spelling—"idiodicy" for "idiocy"—simultaneously commenting on his editorials that simplified complex subjects, particularly the economy, for someone at the level of a typical newspaper reader: an average 12-year-old.

Ted's spelling wasn't conventional, but he could crunch numbers until they were pulverized.

Bingo!

Ted loved math and hated spelling.

I hated math and loved spelling.

We both loved words.

We didn't know it yet, but Fate did: The deal was done and the book was born. Instead of "idiodicy" we would embark on an idea-odyssey, combine assets, and write *Live Debt-Free* . . .

In a few years.

First, another debt-free challenge for me: a house. No more throwing away $110 a month on a cramped apartment's rent.

I'd met the car challenge, saving $2,700 in a year, but I couldn't save cash for a house.

What to do?

Save *some* before buying.

Knowing I'd need at least $5,000 for the down payment to minimize the mortgage, I started squirreling away dollars.

Spring 1975: time to take my $5,000 and find the nicest affordable home possible.

When the Realtor and I spotted a yellow and white house I knew: This was it.

But when she explained the mortgage costs, I suffered first-time buyer's remorse. Could I afford the additional $68 a month for the $178 house payments?

And would I qualify for the loan?

Yes to both.

Because I was debt-free, I was allowed some leeway and sailed through.

After insisting on a clause in the contract permitting me to prepay on the mortgage, I was ready to close in June.

At the closing, paper after paper was pushed toward me.

Was I signing my life away?

The lawyer handed me a final document.

"Here's the mortgage," he said. "It's simple. If you pay, you stay. If you don't, you won't."

Staring at the debt in black and white, I thought: pay/stay, don't/won't. I'd scrimped an extra $800 before the closing so a $20,000 mortgage was reduced to the $19,200 before me. For 30 years, it said, I would pay $178 a month.

No!

I remembered my promise at the joyous celebration in Virginia when we burned the mortgage for the $20,000 house.

Although I still wondered how I'd pay $178 mortgage payments versus the apartment's $110 rent, I was determined. Somehow I would eliminate the mortgage to be debt-free once again.

The math was simple. Paying $178 month by month over three decades, 360 miserable months, would pile up interest.

How high?

How much more would the house cost me if I kept paying for those 30 years?

The $64,000 question became a $64,000 answer.

At $178 for 360 months, my $25,000 house would cost me $64,080.

Oh yeah?

My third-grade self reminded me: "I'm not 'interested' in that!"

I set to work knocking down the principal as fast as possible.

Job security wasn't the best either. If the worst happened and I lost mine, *temporary* interest-only payments wouldn't ruin me; I'd keep the house while I found another job, then resume payoff. Fortunately, I kept my job and slowly but steadily slashed the principal while faithfully paying the $178 per month.

The magic moment came four years to the day after I'd bought my home. I marched into the mortgage company.

The receptionist looked up. "Late payment?"

"No. I'm paying off my mortgage."

Shrugging, she pointed upstairs.

Soon, receipt in hand, I proudly strode down the stairs.

I was debt-free at last!

As I bounded out of the building into the sunshine, I recalled the happy day in Virginia when I hopscotched home from second grade to the scene of the original mortgage burning.

And now it was time for the second of my three $20,000 payoff celebrations.

Paid-off mortgage in hand, I now stood in front of the same fireplace I'd faced as a child. Then, not fully understanding what it meant, I'd celebrated the $20,000 house payoff.

Now it was my show. I would reenact the original celebration with a fire in July. As I threw bits of my mortgage into the flames, I completely understood: I was burning the mortgage and the debt that went with it, saving myself thousands of dollars—*more than 2½ times the original cost of the house.*

I had not only paid for my house while working at *The Times-Union* with Ted. As an added bonus, love had bloomed.

I'd hit the jackpot.

We married and lived the debt-free life together.

Then, ready when a chance presented itself, we bought some land in the country for an eventual house.

Knowing that remaining debt-free would accomplish our goals, we took step one: Clear the land—literally and financially—before building.

For the third of three times, I celebrated a $20,000 payoff as Ted and I threw bits of the mortgage into the fireplace of my long-ago-paid-off Jacksonville house.

Now we prepared to build the country home. Living debt-free on my salary to put Ted's into materials, we worked on a "pay as you build" plan. The house was constructed in stages: foundation, walls and roof, windows and doors, and interior work—with a long break between stages to save more money.

Still debt-free, we left the rat race, big city life, and daily deadline newspaper pressure, where Ted was writing editorials and I was struggling with math in the research department. Ted could write what he *enjoyed* and I'd work with him, editing and writing, too.

Ted laughed. "My father was worried about my spelling. And look. I have a copy editor."

"And," I replied, "I have a mathematician."

We sold our paid-off property—my house in the city, Ted's land—and parlayed the proceeds into a nest egg.

Now, settled debt-free into our cash-built house, we wanted to let others in on our secret and write *Live Debt-Free*. Ted crunched numbers and wrote. I edited and spelled. Everyone was happy.

The book would be fun, with interesting characters illustrating a clear message: You don't have to drown in debt—auto loans, maxed-out credit cards, bank loans, you-name-it loans—*in addition to* the "usual" mortgage.

Who says you *have* to have a mortgage?

Who's "interested" in that?

You can be free of the whole mess.

Don't let the numbers scare you. Ted and I used round numbers—10%, $50,000, and $100,000—as much as possible so you wouldn't be bogged down.

The original version of *Live Debt-Free* was published in 1991. Ever the newspaperman, Ted used the most basic machine to write it: a *manual* typewriter he bought from *The Times-Union*.

No wires.

No plugs.

For those in the computer generation, that means beating on keys with your hands and yanking the carriage across the typewriter—*z-z-z-zip!*—line by line, after the bell rings at the end of each one.

Although he'd used a computer at the newspaper, Ted loved the bell, the noise, and the pounding on the manual typewriter. Another benefit of being debt-free: Ted could use the machine he liked to write what he wanted.

Final revisions of *Live Debt-Free* tested him. We'd moved from the paid-off country house to a debt-free beach condo. Roofers reroofed in the rain, causing a ceiling cave-in and, for us, a move to an oceanfront motel for 3½ weeks.

But a deadline was a deadline. Ted had never missed one. He wouldn't now.

Grabbing his metal typing stand, manual typewriter, and paper, he ignored the ocean's lure and placed the stand, with manual atop it, in the motel room's closet alcove.

Rat-a-tat-tat, ring, yank went the typewriter, with another sound added.

Bang! Against the wall, line by line.

Ted kept at it, working on a simple machine to meet his deadline.

Times, technology, and circumstances have changed in the years since *Live Debt-Free* was originally published.

In 1998, after a productive writing career and a debt-free life, Ted passed away. Because we'd practiced what we'd preached, I was spared one worry: poverty.

I continue to live debt-free so I can take a sunrise walk on the beach and plan my day, a day I've chosen, not one I have to endure because of a debt to a bank, mortgage company, or finance company.

Besides circumstances, technology has advanced considerably. Personal computers have taken over, even for those who used manual typewriters. No more banging out words at a track-and-field-event pace. No more bells and noise.

Times have changed, too. The economy is more volatile than ever. Sometimes I feel as if I'm trying to catch a room full of a million chirping, jumping crickets, one by one, when I read about the latest developments.

But there *is* stability with *Live Debt-Free*. The principle is simple and it holds: No matter what the times, technology, circumstances, or economy, staying out of debt keeps you out of the maelstrom. Whatever happens, you can cope because you're debt-free.

You are holding the updated, expanded version of *Live Debt-Free*.

You have the key to a happy, debt-free life in your hands. All you have to do is unlock the door and walk through.

Happy reading—and *Live Debt-Free*.

—Virginia Carroll, 2003

First Things First

"Money is the most important thing in the world."
—George Bernard Shaw

*L*ive Debt-Free? Is it really possible in this day and age?

As you will see, this book highlights a number of very interesting techniques for managing—and controlling—your financial future. In later chapters of this book, we will look in detail at such issues as how to own your home outright faster than you ever dreamed possible, how to save (painlessly!) on your monthly living expenses, and how to pay a lot less when it comes to your next car. Before we examine these topics, however, it is appropriate to offer some thoughts on taking control of your current income-and-expense picture. That means—hold your breath—taking a look at your budget, or creating one if you do not yet have one.

Your Budget

Your budget is really nothing to be frightened of. What's more frightening is the prospect of working without one. Let's begin by tackling the problem of the person whose debt picture is not a pleasant one—due in no small measure to the fact that he has never constructed a workable budget. We'll call our subject Owen Owing.

Owen is in trouble, and he knows it. His objective is simple: to reach a situation where his monthly income is enough to meet his monthly obligations.

Getting the Numbers

Owen's first step is to identify both expenditures and income available.

It's a simple enough task for Owen to detail his income sources, as it is for most of us. All he has to do is note the amount of pretax earnings on his paycheck. He'll deduct taxes later in the process.

Why not count taxes now? Because they're a payment, like any other payment. Too many people think of their yearly tax refund as a bonus, some fresh bonanza of cash the government is good enough to pass along once a year. Actually, the vast majority of taxpayers—including Owen—are making payments to the taxman with every paycheck. Overpayments, to be precise! Everyone who gets a tax refund has said to the government, "Hold onto this money for a while, take what you need, and give what's left back to me sometime after April 15 every year." It would be nice if Uncle Sam paid us a little interest for the privilege of holding onto our money as long as he does, but sadly, this is not the way things shake out.

So: Taxes are treated as any other expense; Owen lists on a sheet of paper his gross pay, not the amount he takes home. (He would also list any other income sources, such as alimony, child support, or public-assistance payments.)

Next: payment obligations, in monthly amounts. Owen puts them all down on the sheet. (If you're lucky enough to have access to a personal computer and know how to use it, you can incorporate the data on a spreadsheet program rather than bothering with pencils and paper.)

Owen soon faces a problem. What is he supposed to do about the electric bill? That's never the same from month to month. He decides to make his best guess by pulling out a couple of old canceled checks and getting a good middle-of-the-road figure. (You can do the same thing, and with all kinds of bills that have no set amount: phone costs, grocery expenses, and so on.) Similarly, for those bills that come in quarterly or at other nonmonthly intervals, Owen decides to break them down to their monthly equivalents.

Owen takes the same approach for clothing and other purchases he makes on an irregular basis. He makes an educated guess at each such item purchased over the last six months; where necessary, he consults old checks or charge card statements.

This journey down memory lane is a little unsettling for Owen; he's embarrassed to find out how much he actually has spent in some categories over the last half-year. (You might be, too, but avoid the temptation to make the picture look rosier than it really is. You need hard information; and you yourself are the only person who can pull it all together.) Owen gulps, figures out his monthly average spending in all the categories he can think of, and writes everything down.

Owen makes sure he includes costs for travel (including gas, auto repair, subway tokens, and the like); restaurants; entertainment; magazine subscriptions; donations to charitable groups—in short, anything and everything of any consequence. He's careful to avoid lumping lots of things into one category called "Miscellaneous"; he knows that won't give him any meaningful insights on his spending patterns.

He pours himself a cup of coffee, takes a deep breath, and looks at the result of his labors. He knows the picture he's come up with is not an encouraging one—but he pushes on anyway to the next step, categorizing the expenses.

Everything on his sheet fits into one of six categories:

Fixed Expenditures (nondiscretionary)

Items that do not change from month to month and that cannot be removed easily from the budget.

Examples:
- Rent or fixed-rate mortgage
- Car payments
- Insurance premiums

Fixed Expenses (discretionary)

Items that do not change from month to month and that could be removed from the budget without extraordinary difficulty.

Examples:
- Newspaper subscriptions
- Monthly dues to social organizations
- Health club membership

Variable Expenditures (nondiscretionary)

Items that vary every month and that cannot be removed easily from the budget.

Examples:
- Utility bills
- Telephone bill
- Grocery expenses

Variable Expenses (discretionary)

Items that vary from month to month and that could be removed from the budget without extraordinary difficulty.

Examples:
- Restaurant expenses
- Theater or movie tickets
- Prerecorded music and movies (compact discs, DVDs)

Repayments

Loans on household items bought previously on credit. Usually fixed amounts.

Example:
- Household appliances bought "on time"

Taxes

Examples:
- State and federal withholding taxes
- Social Security payments

Here's how Owen's first analysis came out.

Owen's Average Monthly Financial Picture
Based on January through June expenses

Salary (4 weeks)	$3,846.00

Fixed Expenditures (nondiscretionary)

Car payment	$372.27
Car insurance	$104.00
Life insurance	$100.00
Mortgage	$1,278.67
Student loan	$268.74

Fixed Expenses (discretionary)

Cable	$57.25
Health club membership	$40.00
Subscriptions	$17.25

Variable Expenditures (nondiscretionary)
Estimates based on past records:

Clothing	$192.87
Electricity	$95.67
Groceries	$216.38
Telephone	$62.87

Variable Expenses (discretionary)
Estimates based on past records:

Books	$68.27
Gifts	$52.00
Movies/videos	$33.60
Online computer service	$21.95
Restaurants	$102.14
Theater	$25.20

Repayments

Credit cards (minimum due)	$236.78
Personal computer and equipment	$82.67
Stereo	$53.14
TV	$37.63

Taxes

Federal withholding	$423.06
Social Security	$153.84
State withholding	$115.38
TOTAL:	$4,211.63
Owen's Average End-of-Month Position:	–$365.63

Ouch! As painful as that picture is to look at, Owen realizes that ignoring it is only going to lead to further trouble. The question now is: How does he go about setting up the new budget—the one that will get him out of this mess?

He takes a long look at the two "discretionary" categories—the lists of items he has admitted to himself are nonessentials. There is a certain amount of judgment involved here; he might have considered his mortgage to be a discretionary item if he felt he could sell his house and move in with his mother and father again!

Now: Which of the items on these two lists would be easiest to do without for a while? After a little thought, the conclusions start coming. Perhaps a couple of softcover books at $9.95 each would be acceptable for a few months, rather than the hardcover editions Owen is used to. And the health club—that's certainly no crime to cancel, at least temporarily. He'll jog at the park instead. The magazine subscriptions: Does he actually *read* what he receives?

Of course, there are other places to cut back besides the "discretionary" categories. Owen really had no idea how much he was spending on clothes—it won't be too difficult for him to reduce his purchases in that area through a little more prudent shopping. He finds there are a number of items like this.

And the "repayments" category: What about that? Well, if he could get away without touching those, he would—but it looks like he might have to do some prioritizing. His first objective is to keep making credit card payments on time; failing to do so is the surest way to a bad credit rating, and he doesn't want that. He decides to try to work out new terms on some of the home entertainment and computer equipment—*before* his account goes past due. (You can often renegotiate such agreements, although it might take some perseverance. The key is to head off trouble ahead of time.)

After an hour or so of such analysis, Owen comes up with another budget. Compare the one that follows to his first one!

Owen's Monthly Financial Targets

Salary (4 weeks)	$3,846.00

Fixed Expenditures (nondiscretionary)

Car payment	$372.27
Car insurance	$104.00
Life insurance	$100.00
Mortgage	$1,278.67
Student loan	$268.74

Fixed Expenses (discretionary)

Cable	$00.00

Health club membership	$00.00
Subscriptions (newspaper only)	$10.50

Variable Expenditures (nondiscretionary)
Estimates based on past records:

Clothing	$85.00
Electricity	$95.67
Groceries	$170.00
Telephone (watch long distance)	$45.00

Variable Expenses (discretionary)
Estimates based on past records:

Books	$20.00
Gifts	$12.00
Movies/videos	$15.00
Online computer service	$9.95
Restaurants	$50.00
Theater	$00.00

Repayments

Credit cards (minimum due)	$236.78
Personal computer and equipment (renegotiate)	$50.00
Stereo (renegotiate)	$40.00
TV (renegotiate)	$25.00

Taxes

Federal withholding	$423.06
Social Security	$153.84
State withholding	$115.38

TOTAL:	$3,680.86
Owen's Projected End-of-Month Position:	$165.14

Of course, it all looks good on paper—but execution is another matter. It will be important for Owen to follow through on his planning by monitoring his expenses closely, and that will require discipline. Specifically, it will require keeping track of things in an expense log. Many people wonder if they will be able to adapt to the "shackles" of an expense log—but the true shackles are the monthly bills that pile up and cannot be paid. After a few months of monitoring things closely, Owen will be in a position to take advantage of the imaginative techniques outlined elsewhere in this book—and you will, too.

CHAPTER TWO

Do You Run Your Life or Do Your Creditors?

"I have been poor and I have been rich. Rich is better."
—*Sophie Tucker*

"Fly now, pay later" has become the basic building block of our society. Open any newspaper to the auto ads and you may see: "Only $199 a month" in a typical headline. Hold on to your magnifying glass and you might eventually, with patience, learn the price of the car somewhere in the fine print.

And it's not only big-ticket items that promise "easy" payments:

- Blared a department store ad in *September,* "Buy Now. No payment 'til *next February!*"
- Junk mail peddling flatware table services bragged, "Only six payments of just $4.62 each!" For—would you believe—a $19.99 purchase!
- The cheese catalogues arriving in time for Christmas shout, "no payments 'til next year"; and some will kindly allow you to make 10 monthly installments on your gift boxes.

- And there are those mail-order magazine subscription houses that show the price of a subscription in small type while headlines boast, "As little as $1.99 a month on our four-pay plan!"

Next time you buy a soft drink out of a machine, will a charge slip fall out to let you pay next month in four weekly installments?

Let's get one thing straight. I would never be so preposterous as to ask anyone to forego the convenience of credit cards, paid in full monthly, so that no interest is involved. Major credit cards are a convenient bonus of today's society. They are better than cash and no one should be without them. (Later on, I'll tell you about a man who built his house on VISA!) Nor will this book ramble on about the horrors of today's mortgage jungles, such as those tricky little variable rate deals that jump again before you've quit cussing the last jump, balloon notes, or the fixed-payment variable rate mortgage, which can lead you into negative amortization—meaning that after 30 years of payments you could conceivably owe more than you borrowed originally!

I also won't:

- Ask you to struggle, scrimp, deny yourself, and sacrifice for endless years to "get ahead."
- Tell you to drive yourself nuts clipping coupons on stuff you don't want anyway or filling out 20-page affidavits to get a $1 manufacturer's refund.
- Suggest that you invest in any suspicious "get-rich-quick" schemes.

Of course, if you like clipping coupons (some people do and

they do save money)—enjoy. What I'm trying to say is that while such stuff fills some "save money" books, it's not the issue here.

This is what I *will* show you:

- Simple ways you can resume control of your financial situation—control you might have to win back from creditors a step at a time.
- How you can live in your dream home, in your dream neighborhood, without spending the better part of your life paying interest to the bank.
- How you can get the car you've always wanted—interest-free.

Much more important—I will show you how, once freed from the economic treadmill upon which so many millions spend their lives, you can take command of your life and live it according to your own values.

CHAPTER THREE

The Own-Your-Home-Sooner Plan

"Money is like an arm or a leg—use it or lose it."
—Henry Ford

Let's watch two nice young couples go house hunting. Meet couple number one: We'll call them Al and Alice Interestpayer. And couple number two: We'll call them Sam and Sue Sharp.

They have a lot in common: Both couples are up-and-coming go-getters in their mid-twenties; both are prudently waiting a while before starting a family; both are two-paycheckers with around $80,000 annual income per couple; both have $20,000 in savings for a down payment plus enough in checking for closing costs; both, therefore, can afford a $200,000 mortgage. The difference is, Al and Alice Interestpayer haven't read this book. Sam and Sue Sharp have.

$ 🐸 $

Al and Alice have a heart-to-heart talk with Mr. Jolly, the real estate salesman.

"This might be the house we'll live in for the rest of our lives," Alice explains. "So we want a nice neighborhood."

Smiling, they climb into Jolly's Mercedes and go tooling around town and countryside. Al thumps walls to the hollow ring of Sheetrock as Alice goes "oooh" and "ahhh" at chrome kitchen fixtures and pine hardwood floors. On their third house-hunting day, they turn onto a shady street and get that "this is it" feeling.

"You'll have your choice," says Jolly. "Across the street from each other: the split-level with brown-stained shingles over brick, or the yellow stucco Spanish-style one-story. The price is the same: $220,000." Al and Alice walk back and forth across the street several times. Both exclaim, "I like the neighborhood!"

"The Spanish one is a charmer," says Alice.

"The split level has more room," says Al.

"You're right. Let's take it."

Al and Alice sign on the line, and the next day Jolly whisks them into an even jollier banker's inner sanctum. Papers are signed for a $200,000 mortgage—coffee is on the house.

"In just 30 years," jokes Alice as they leave, "it will be ours."

$ 🐷 $

Sam and Sue sing a different tune. They ask a lot more of their real estate salesman, chosen because he has a reputation as a hard worker.

"You'll have to work to meet our specifications," Sam speaks candidly to the salesman, Mr. Worker. "We have a flat budget limit of $120,000."

"Well . . . ," the hard-working salesman hesitates, "you won't find many houses in this area for that money, but we'll do the best we can."

"I haven't finished," Sam grins. "It must also have strong resale value. We'll be selling in about five years."

"We realize it will have to be a small place," Sue adds. "But we want it to be a fun place to live. Some friends of ours bought a small condo for that price. It overlooks the river, and they have dock space."

Worker drums his fingers on his small salesman's desk. "I can show you a townhouse, small, but close to everything. Say, there's a honeymoon cottage on the edge of town that used to be the caretaker's house on an estate. Shall we look?"

They did; half a dozen places on the first weekend. Sue loved an artist's studio converted to a residence: The two-story living room, rising to a skylight, had a sleeping loft at one end and a log-burning fireplace at the other. But in the end, they settled on a rustic log cabin outside town, surrounded by towering oaks and facing a lake. It was small, having originally been a fishing cabin, and picturesque; they loved it.

"In a couple of years," their real estate agent said, "a new manufacturing plant will open three miles from here. That should give great resale prospects." That settled it.

The next day, Sam and Sue signed on the line for *their* mortgage. Their payments were practically the same as Al and Alice's. Half the house for the same payment? Sure. Believe me, Sam and Sue know what they're doing!

$ 🏠 $

Five years later, Sam and Sue began house hunting again. They went with the same salesman, Worker, since he had tried so hard for them before.

"This time around," Sam said, "our limit is $240,000."

On day four the salesman drove them to a tree-lined street with a yellow stucco Spanish-style one-story for sale.

"Say," Sam remarked as they got out, "that's Al Interestpayer raking leaves across the street in front of that split-level. He works at the same place I do."

Sue was excited about the house even before they entered. They walked around and around, pointing and talking. The next day they came back and looked for an hour.

"The price," the salesman said, "seems within your limit. I'm sure we can get it for $240,000."

"We'll take it."

Then Sam and Sue went to the bank for their new mortgage.

$ 🏠 $

Time passed.

Ten years after Al and Alice and Sam and Sue bought their first homes, along came a bitter winter afternoon. Two entirely different kinds of family events took place in the split-level and the Spanish house across the street. Al and Alice, going over piled-up bills, looked at their amortization schedule, noting that they had 20 more years—240 more months—of payments. Sam and Sue listened to the pop of the champagne cork and shot off fireworks on the patio as they burned their mortgage in the barbecue pit. "Our home is free and clear! Hallelujah!" they sang out.

For the next two decades, the money that would have been going to the bank for mortgage principal and interest will stay with Sam and Sue. They can spend or invest, as they choose, live it up in the present, and/or pave the road to future comfort and security.

$ 🏠 $

You have just witnessed, in action, the Own-Your-Home-Sooner Plan's basic principle: *Within the contemporary range of interest rate fluctuations, approximately the same monthly payment that would pay off a $200,000 mortgage in 30 years will pay off a*

$100,000 mortgage in about five years—and thus $200,000 in mortgages (two $100,000 mortgages) in about 10 years.

This principle holds, with minor variations, as mortgage rates go up and down. In recent years, interest has ranged as low as 5% and as high as 18%. The consensus is that such instability will continue.

Interest Rates

Nobody can predict the prevailing interest rate at the moment this book reaches your hands, but while the numbers will differ, the principle remains the same.

The figures will differ as interest rates fluctuate, but not nearly as much as you might think. For example, let's take the monthly principal and interest payments for Al and Alice and for Sam and Sue at rates ranging from 5% to 15%. Remember, mortgage payments typically consist of four factors: loan principal, loan interest, escrow for property taxes, and escrow for property insurance. Taxes and insurance will always be paid on the property and are separate from any principal and interest calculations throughout this book.

At 5% interest, Al and Alice would pay $1,074 monthly. (For simplicity, all figures will be rounded off to the nearest dollar throughout this book.) Sam and Sue pay $1,887. The lower the interest, the more the advantage seems to tip toward Al and Alice—*over the short haul.* However, it must be remembered that the monthly mortgage check includes an escrow for taxes and insurance as well as the principal and interest payment. Keeping in mind that for the first five years Sam and Sue will be paying on a $120,000 property rather than a $200,000 property, and since taxes and insurance are roughly proportionate to value, Al and Alice will be paying about twice the insurance and tax escrow. Thus, in a low-tax area Sam and Sue might pay a little more monthly overall than Al and Alice, while in a high-tax area Al and Alice could pay more every month from the start. Tax rates vary so widely that there is no way to generalize.

At 10% interest, Sam and Sue will pay $2,125 a month on principal and interest, compared to Al and Alice's $1,755. Again, the escrow could roughly equalize the overall payments the first five years. But by the 15% mark, Al and Alice *always* pay more in principal and interest than Sam and Sue, not even counting the escrow. Al and Alice's principal and interest tab is $2,528, compared to Sam and Sue's $2,379.

> At 5%: Al and Alice pay $1,074 monthly, compared to $1,887 for Sam and Sue.
>
> At 10%: Al and Alice pay $1,755 monthly, compared to $2,125 for Sam and Sue.
>
> At 15%: Al and Alice pay $2,528 monthly, compared to $2,379 for Sam and Sue.

Let's assume, for simplicity, a middle-range figure of 10% interest on all consumer loans. We will also assume a rate of 8% for all money invested as a mid-range figure. Of course, you can beat that; just about anyone can. This figure is merely to illustrate the principle. Now a quick summary.

At the presumed 10% interest, Sam and Sue put up $20,000 cash and take a $100,000 mortgage on their first house, the "log cabin." They pay this off in five years. Now they next find that "big house," the one that will be their permanent home. They'll put the money from the first sale into the second house and wind up with another five-year loan—making 10 years in all.

Then they are free forever of mortgage payments.

As for Al and Alice, they'll pay the first 10 years, as Sam and Sue do; then Al and Alice will pay for 20 years—240 monthly payments—more. The monthly payment rundown, of course, is far from the whole story. Reflect for a moment upon the *total* that our two couples will pay for their identically priced houses (not including each couple's identical $20,000 down payment):

At 5%: Al and Alice $386,510 compared to $226,455 for Sam and Sue

At 10%: Al and Alice $631,850 compared to $254,965 for Sam and Sue

At 15%: Al and Alice $910,400 compared to $285,479 for Sam and Sue

Sam and Sue are far less at the mercy of the current interest rate than are Al and Alice. This is because even skyrocketing interest rates don't affect short-term borrowing anywhere near as much as long-term borrowing. It really does not matter so much if the interest is 5% or 10% or 15%. The important point is that Sam and Sue will keep, for their own use, 240 payments—one each month for 20 long years—while Al and Alice are still writing checks to the bank. Sam and Sue's eventual principal and interest savings might be $1,887 monthly (at 5%) or $2,379 (at 15%), but it's still "found money" as far as they are concerned.

This monthly $2,000, more or less, is the basis of Sam and Sue's financial freedom and control of their lifestyles—as it can be for you, too.

Questions and Answers

Q: You're forgetting inflation. The house that cost $210,000 five years ago could cost a lot more money today.

A: Inflation simply isn't a big deal when using this plan. Sure, prices rise in the five-year period: The $210,000 house Sam and Sue are buying will go, say, to $230,000; the $110,000 house they are selling will likewise rise to $121,000. Actually, since this concept specifically calls for buying the first house *with an eye to resale value*, rather than long-term livability, the smaller house could increase, in dollars, even more than the larger house. At any rate, when considering resale value, remember that you must keep pace with inflation. Think in terms of what we call "hamburger dollars." You buy a house for, say, $100,000 when a hamburger costs $1. Down the road of time your house sells for $200,000— when hamburgers cost $2. You have not made $100,000 "profit" on your house: You have simply gone from $100,000 hamburgers' worth of house A to $100,000 hamburgers' worth of house B.

Q: In the past, interest rates have skyrocketed, and this could happen again. Suppose Sam and Sue buy their first house at 5% interest, but when they go to buy their second house, the interest rate has shot sky-high to 10%—twice as high. Won't this throw the whole plan out the window?

A: You are absolutely right that this could happen again, but you'd be surprised how little it affects the basic principle. At 5%, the principal and interest payments for the first house would be $1,887 monthly. At 10% for the second loan, this figure would, true, jump to $2,125. But the difference between the two interest rates over just five years is only $14,280. Meanwhile Sam and Sue's total payment will still be less than $255,000 on both loans, whereas financing for 30 years, as Al and Alice did back when the interest rate was only 5%, would mean paying more than $386,000 for the house—a difference of more than $131,000.

Q: Aren't you overlooking the real estate commission and closing costs on the house Sam and Sue are selling?

A: Actually, these costs are simply insignificant in the overall picture. Don't sweat the small stuff!

Q: Your plan specifies paying each mortgage in about five years. In my area, banks write mortgages for a minimum of 10 years. How can I get around this?

A: It doesn't matter—as long as you have the right to prepay without penalty (never get a loan without this provision). Then work out your own schedule to retire the loan in five years rather than the 10 or 20 or 30 years provided. Simply prepay enough each month to equal a five-year principal and interest amortization, making whole principal prepayments to keep the schedule straight.

Q: Aren't you forgetting the tax angle?

A: The road to many a personal economic hell has been paved with those well-intended words, "but it's deductible!" Your concern isn't with how many pennies you can get back on dollars you have gratuitously thrown away, but the total number of dollars you can keep.

Current tax laws make this plan even more favorable; why throw away whole dollars so that you can deduct, at best, 28 cents? Because of tax bracket changes, interest deductions may mean less for you than they used to. Taking the standard deduction for couples (currently $7,850) puts most families who don't pay interest well ahead, not to mention not having to struggle with substantiating all deductions. Consult your tax advisor to discuss how this plan could affect you.

Q: You seem to be talking about yuppie couples making $80,000 a year and buying $210,000 homes. What good is your plan to a good ole country boy (or girl) who lives in a low-income area and brings home little more than the minimum wage?

A: The principle of *Live Debt-Free* applies regardless of income level or housing prices. In areas with low-income rates, the real estate market is in proportion. So suppose Joe and Jody have, together, about $500 in take-home pay per week. They can likely find a clean, small trailer with a lot for $20,000 to $25,000—take $22,000 as a mid-range figure for low-cost housing in rural areas.

At 10% for five years of payments with $1,000 down and a mortgage of $21,000, payments for principal and interest will be $446. Taxes would be low (in some states, Florida, for example, the homestead exemption would eliminate *all* taxes), and so would insurance. Joe and Jody could swing it and watch the sun rise over the distant pines from their breakfast table.

Then step up to the second home; a $50,000 double-wide or small cabin on a larger lot, for another five years of payments within their means.

The truth is, the lower the income, the more important every household dollar becomes; every dime must do its duty. Thus, mortgage-free living after 10 years or so could be an even greater boon to Joe and Jody than to their more affluent urban counterparts.

Unforeseen Crises

Let's forget statistics a moment and think of some not-so-nice things that can and do happen to nice people. Let's imagine that the computer manufacturer, where Al and Sam both work, closes without warning, just four years after Al and Sam bought houses. And, since plants throughout that entire industry are folding instead of opening, job prospects seem nil.

Al and Alice hold their wake at the supper table.

"What are we gonna do, honey?" asks Alice.

"One thing's sure, we can't keep up these house payments."

"At least we ought to have some equity. Let me get that table thing, so we can see what we still owe."

Al studies the amortization table. "I must be looking at the wrong place," he says.

It takes a few minutes for Al and Alice to understand that (a) Al is looking at the right place and (b) their "equity" in their home, after 48 payments totaling more than $84,240 for principal and interest, is only a little more than $5,000. As the sun sets, Al and Alice slouch sadly on the porch they had so loved, which they had thought would be theirs forever.

"We'll have to sell in a hurry or else lose the house and get a bad credit rating to boot," Al says. "After we pay real estate commission and closing costs, we probably won't even get our $20,000 down payment back."

The next morning Al calls a real estate broker and Alice

sets out to look for (her words) "some crummy apartment."

Of course, life could hand Al and Alice a different kind of bombshell. Look at the statistics: Half of today's marriages end in divorce. So suppose that, instead of Al losing his job, Al and Alice decide to split—say, eight years after they bought their house.

Al looks to the amortization table. "I can hardly believe it," he says. "By now we've paid in more than $168,000 on principal and interest but we've got less than $13,000 equity. We will owe $187,066. It doesn't seem possible!" But, of course, it is. And while the house has appreciated some, there will still be practically nothing left after selling costs—"maybe a couple of thousand apiece when we split." And so to domestic discord add one memorable knockdown drag-out money fight.

Since we're supposing, why not reflect upon the ultimate disaster—that all is well with Al and Alice until one night, 14 years after Al and Alice settled into their dream home, an uninsured drunk driver runs into Al on his way home, and Al becomes another highway fatality statistic. Now Alice is not only a widow in emotional distress, she has sudden financial problems as well. She tears up the house to find the amortization table, only to discover that—although they indeed have paid $294,800 in principal and interest—she still owes $167,811!

Now let's look at Sam and Sue. Suppose the same hardship, personal disaster, or tragedy happens to them. Sam has a long look on his face when he tells Sue about the plant closing after they have been in their first house four years. But he cheers up, looking at their amortization table. "We only owe $24,167 on our mortgage," he says. "That gives us $75,833 equity, and the house is worth more than we paid."

"Let's just relax and figure things out," suggests Sue.

The next morning, over a leisurely breakfast they look over

the lake and, braced by steaming cups of coffee, ponder their alternatives.

"We could sell and pay cash for a 'double-wide' in the neighborhood," Sam says. "Without house payments to make, we could make it on your salary easily for a while."

"Or we could get a one-bedroom condo in the city, a small one like the Smiths have."

"I kind of like the country best," Sam says.

"You're right," Sue agrees. "I'd much rather stay here too."

"Say," Sam adds, "we can even stay right here. There's enough equity so we can refinance temporarily, until I get a job—then we can get back on schedule."

Again, suppose it's Sam and Sue who, at the eight-year point, agree to disagree. They have just finished the third year's payments on their second home.

Sam checks the figures. "It's worth at least the $210,000 we paid," he says. "We owe under $47,000. Even after selling costs, it'll be a walloping equity—around $71,000 to $72,000 apiece."

Sue nods, semi-sadly. For, though love may have departed, at least there's enough capital around to ease the financial pains.

Again, think tragic.

Fourteen years after they bought their first house—four years after they burned the mortgage on their dream home—Sam falls victim to an uninsured drunk driver. As Sue bravely assesses her situation, she reflects that, at least, her home is paid—a potential nest egg should she decide to sell. And in addition there will be, on hand, as much as they had saved of the money not paid to the bank each month for the last four years, saved at 8% interest, more than $110,000.

$ 🐍 $

Life may run smoothly. You may never have any problems. But before you count on it, why not ask about the odds? Readers of this book who were born after World War II may have never experienced truly "hard times." Even so, one doesn't have to look back to the Great Depression to realize that life does not always run without a hitch—even such a "minor" one as the Dow Jones average dropping more than 500 points in a day.

Remember the aerospace engineers who won the space race for us and became celebrated national heroes? A grateful nation promptly rewarded them by kicking them out of their jobs by the thousands. Scientists and engineers, many of them with Ph.D.s, who had been making $35,000 or $45,000 a year (lots of money way back then) couldn't even find jobs as soda jerks at the minimum wage. Remember the Detroit auto workers who were laid off—despite a strong union—by the tens of thousands and eventually hundreds of thousands, as Japanese imports flooded American streets. Or look at the havens of the hi-tech industry, as dozens of firms were squeezed out by a slumping market. Vocational experts forecast that the young adult entering the job market today will change his or her field of work—not just employer but the *kind of work* done—six times before retirement. Even the mighty fall, and sometimes they fall the hardest; high-salaried executives are often the first to go when a company is sold or merged.

So hope that all runs smoothly in the years ahead—but remember to ask yourself, now, well in advance: If misfortune does strike, would you rather be like Al and Alice—or Sam and Sue?

CHAPTER FOUR

A Buyer's Guide to First-Time Homebuying

"Money makes the world go 'round."
—*Cabaret* (1970)

Here, based in part on the article *Wise Home Buying* from the U.S. Department of Housing and Urban Development (HUD), is some practical advice on how much home you can afford; what to look for in a home (to save now and later); and how and where to get financing.

All of the advice works within the *Live Debt-Free* plan, which is designed to allow you to pay off two mortgages—and live debt-free—within 10 years.

$ 💰 $

Perhaps your first consideration is the matter of paying for a new home. Here are two methods many people use to estimate ability to meet house payments.

1. The price of the home generally should not exceed two times your annual family income. Of course, under the

debt-free plan, you are buying a house at half the price you are eligible to buy, so that is no problem.

2. A homeowner usually should not pay more than the family's weekly income after federal tax for monthly housing expense (payment on the mortgage loan plus average cost of heat, utilities, repair, and maintenance).

The buyer should have the cash necessary to meet the down payment and other expenses at closing time. Ask your real estate salesperson or lender to provide an estimate of all closing costs you will need at the time of settlement.

How to Find the Right House

Your first home is the cornerstone of the *Live Debt-Free* approach, so choose carefully. There are various ways to shop for the house that is right for your family. Houses are sold chiefly through real estate advertising and real estate brokers. Sometimes they can be purchased directly from the owners.

Read the advertisements in real estate sections of local newspapers.

Tell your friends and neighbors that you are house hunting. Then take your time in shopping the market. Don't quit until you have a clear idea of the cost and quality of homes currently offered for sale.

Take a Sunday afternoon drive or walk through the neighborhoods you find attractive. You may locate houses that are offered for sale and model homes on display.

Don't trust your memory when you find an appealing house: Keep a record listing the asking price, owner's name, location, number of bedrooms, taxes, heating bills, and any special features. An inexpensive notebook is all you need.

What Real Estate Brokers Do

Many homeseekers ask, "Should I use the services of a real estate broker?"

In most cases using a real estate broker will be to your advantage. A good real estate broker provides a clearing center for marketable houses, and his screening process will save you many a wild goose chase.

Multiple listing services offered by a broker will give a better understanding of housing areas and price ranges.

A good broker will give you general information about a community and specific information about schools, churches, and stores. He may be able to help you get financing and may know how to eliminate much red tape.

The broker's commission is usually 6% of the sales price but can reach 7% in some areas. This commission is paid by the party or parties who engage the broker, usually the seller of the house.

To find a good real estate broker, ask your friends or call the mortgage officers of local banks and savings-and-loan associations. Notice which brokers run the most newspaper advertisements for houses in the neighborhoods you prefer. Often brokers will specialize in a particular neighborhood.

One bit of cautious advice: Do not rely on oral promises or agreements. Remember, the broker is usually working principally for a seller, not a buyer. If you want a broker who will look out for your interests, look for a broker who works as a "buyer's broker" to help you in your house search.

New House or Used?

Statistics show that two out of every three buyers select a used house. The one person out of three who buys a new house is likely to purchase one that is already built rather than to build his own house or have one built. This is a choice each home-buyer must make for himself. Usually one of the biggest advantages that an older house offers is more space for the money. The lot may have been planted with trees and shrubs by previous owners and therefore presents relatively few landscaping problems. In an established neighborhood taxes are usually stable. And don't fail to weigh the possibility of shorter commuting times and distances from an older neighborhood to schools, offices, and other frequent destinations. Future road construction also could affect the value of a home, so you may wish to check plans for construction with local authorities.

Before purchasing a house in an older neighborhood, be sure that you check on any future plans for neighborhood improvement, urban renewal, or land appropriation for new highways or other projects.

Many older homes have ample bedroom space and this is an important fact in choosing a house. Observe how the floor space has been used by the builder. Most buyers will prefer a house containing fewer rooms that are spacious and livable to a house with a larger number of small cell-like rooms.

Remember, under the *Live Debt-Free* plan, you are aiming to pay for and sell your first house in five years. So take your preferences—and those of most potential homebuyers—into consideration. They may affect the potential resale value of your home.

An Older Home

Choosing an older or newer home is a matter of personal preference and makes little difference under the *Live Debt-Free* plan. But each choice contains potential risks. And taking care of problems up front will reduce your costs later on.

With an older home, what first appears to be a bargain home may turn out to be a headache. A thorough inspection may reveal hidden defects and obvious remodeling needs.

Few people make a full-time business of checking house construction. To eliminate any doubts about the soundness of the house you have selected, obtain an expert appraisal of the property to establish its value and point out deficiencies. In many cities there are reputable inspection firms that will examine the home and give you a detailed report. The fee can range from $150 to over $500, but the money may be well spent. Some buyers face the expense of replacing basic equipment within the first year of ownership. If you have doubts about the wiring, plumbing, or heating plant, the owner should permit you to have it checked by an expert.

If the plumbing system includes a septic tank, an expert should check the equipment before you purchase.

If you must call in experts, first check their reputations and beware of unscrupulous operators who may justify their fee by exaggerating flaws that they want to repair at inflated costs.

If it appears that repairs and improvements are needed, be sure to secure estimates in advance of the cost of the work and find out who will pay for it—you or the seller.

Older houses deserve special attention in nine areas before a prospective buyer signs on the dotted line. So check these items carefully.

1. *Termite infestation and wood rot.* The importance of a check for termites cannot be overemphasized, particularly in those areas of the country that have a history of infestation. It is generally wise to include a termite clause in the contract, which gives certification of termite inspection and guarantee.

2. *Structural failure.* Examine the construction for a sagging roof, cracked walls or slabs, uneven floors, or other evidence of supporting soil or poor bearing capacity or inadequate structural members.

3. *Inadequate wiring.* Be sure that there is sufficient amperage and enough electric outlets. Request inspection by the local government for code compliance to make sure the wiring is not dilapidated, exposed, and dangerous.

4. *Run-down heating plant.* Check the general condition of the heating system. What kind of repairs are needed and how long will the system last?

5. *Inadequate insulation.* Ask if the attic and the space between interior and exterior walls have been filled with an insulating material. What material was used and how was it installed?

6. *Faulty plumbing.* Choose a home that is connected to a public sewer system in preference to one served by a septic tank or a cesspool. Check with the plumber who last serviced the house to determine condition of the plumbing and ask him to test for water pressure.

7. *Hot-water heater.* Check the type and capacity of the tank to determine if there will be sufficient hot water for family needs. Look for any signs of rust or leaks. Obtain any guarantee held by the present owner, if it is still in effect.

8. *Roof and gutters.* What kind of roofing material was used and how old is it? Check inside the attic for water stains and discoloration. Ask the owner for a guarantee if one exists.

9. *Wet basements.* A basement that looks dry in summer may be four inches under water in the spring. Are there signs around the foundation walls of water penetration?

Inadequacies in the above items can and should reduce the price of the house.

Examine the conditions of the outside paint and the paint and wallpaper inside the house. Be sure all windows and doors operate and are in repair. If there is a fireplace, it should have a workable damper. Inspect floor and wall tile and fixtures in the bathroom. Determine if the attic has sufficient storage area.

Remember, there is no perfect house. Just be sure you know in advance the shortcomings of the house you are buying. Don't wait to be shocked after you move in.

A New House

If, after weighing all the factors, you decide that a new home will best meet your needs, make certain that you make the best buy by following these helpful rules.

The reliability of the builder is an important consideration in choosing a new home. A reputable builder is in business for life. Arrange to talk with people who are living in houses constructed by the builder you are considering. When you've decided on the builder, consider these points:

1. Don't be overwhelmed by the appearance of a glittering model home. Pin down exactly which features are provided with your new house and which are "extras" displayed in the model.
2. Be sure the contract is complete and that there is agreement on all the details of the transactions. Don't assume an item is included and later discover you've misunderstood.
3. If the community is to have new street paving, water and sewer lines, and sidewalks, make sure you know

whether you or the builder will assume the costs. Find out about charges for water and trash collection.

4. Check the lot size in advance. Is it the size and setting you want for your home? After the bulldozer has arrived, it may be too late.

5. Don't take anyone else's word about the zoning uses permitted for the area in which you plan to buy a home. The neighborhood may be strictly residential or zoned for certain commercial uses. This information could affect future property values. The city, county, or township clerk's office can tell you where to inquire about zoning.

6. The contract with the builder should set forth the total sales price. If possible, try to locate a lender who will allow you to take advantage of lower interest rates which may apply at the time of closing. In any event, avoid an arrangement which would allow the lender to increase the mortgage interest rate if market conditions change between the date of the mortgage commitment and the closing date.

7. Be sure your contract with the builder definitely stipulates the completion date of your home.

8. Don't be afraid to check construction progress regularly while the house is being built.

9. Any extra features that are to be included in the finished house should be described in writing.

10. The day before you take title to the house (closing day), make a thorough inspection trip. Check all equipment, windows, and doors. This is your last chance to request changes.

11. Insist on these papers when you take possession: (a) warranties from all manufacturers for equipment in the

house; (b) certificate of occupancy; and (c) certificates from the Health Department clearing plumbing and sewer installations. It would also be best to obtain all applicable certificates of code compliance.

Financing and Purchasing

This is one of the most important elements in living debt-free. Why? Because by selecting a suitable financing plan, you will be able to get out from under your debt more quickly.

There are a number of ways to finance the purchase of a home. One, of course, is payment of the whole price in cash, but most people purchase by obtaining a long-term mortgage loan requiring a down payment—usually 5% to 20% of the price, followed by monthly mortgage payments of principal, interest, taxes, and property insurance.

Also, you may assume and agree to pay the remaining mortgage debt on an existing house. This method has several advantages. The closing cost will be considerably lower, the interest rate on the old mortgage may be lower than the current rate for a new mortgage, and the transaction can be closed faster.

When placing a sales contract on a home, the buyer is usually required to deposit a nominal sum as earnest money. The house is then taken off the selling market until approved financing can be arranged. This earnest money deposit is forfeited to the seller if the purchaser defaults in carrying out the contract.

How to Shop for Mortgage Money

Whether you choose a long-term bank mortgage or an assumable mortgage, you should try to reduce your upfront costs as much as possible. This is especially true of points, the charges assessed by banks as part of the closing costs, which can run as high as 3.5% of the sales price of the home. By selecting a mortgage with fewer points, you may be charged a high rate of interest. But, because you are paying off the mortgage quickly, you will be able to save money, even with a slightly higher interest rate.

Also, be certain that your mortgage allows you to make the extra payments to reduce your principal. Most do. But be certain. This is the basis for living debt-free.

In very simple terms, a mortgage loan is a special loan for purchasing a piece of property. The lender supplies cash to buy the house. The borrower (mortgagor) signs a legal document which obligates and binds him to repay the lender (mortgagee) regular payments, including interest for a specified number of years. The house and lot are pledged as security and the borrower promises to pay the taxes, keep the house insured, and maintain the property in good condition. If the borrower fails to make payments (defaults), the lender has the legal right to take over the property and the borrower may lose any equity he has acquired.

When selecting a mortgage be sure you understand the terms of your mortgage loan. Will your monthly payment change? If it does change, is it according to a predetermined schedule or are changes dependent upon a certain index?

Find out how often the monthly payment can change and whether or not there is a maximum amount it can be increased or decreased. You should understand what effect the changes in monthly payments might have on the mortgage amount you are obligated to repay.

Sometimes the seller of the house will offer to provide financing by holding or "taking back" a mortgage. In such a situation, the term of the mortgage is often less than the amortization period, requiring you to obtain financing to pay the seller when the note is due.

You may ask, "How and where do I obtain a mortgage loan?"

Mortgage loans are obtained from savings banks, commercial banks, savings and loan associations, mortgage bankers, insurance companies, and relatives. Shop around and compare, and find where you can secure a mortgage loan on the best terms for your financial condition.

You will find the banking and savings and loan institutions ready to work with you. This is their business. Local mortgage brokers and insurance company offices are also possibilities.

If you contact your relatives, be sure to keep the deal on a firm business basis. It is important that you leave nothing to verbal agreement. The fine print is just as important dealing with a relative or friend as in dealing with a stranger or a large, impersonal firm.

Each of the mortgage sources mentioned may provide a conventional mortgage loan or one insured by the Department of Housing and Urban Development (HUD) or guaranteed by the Veterans Administration, if you are an eligible veteran.

The Buyer's Obligation

The homebuyer who contracts for a loan obligates himself to make monthly payments on time. Like other debts, he is required to meet these payments whether or not he likes certain features of the home. If the home is new, he can contact the builder to remedy defects reasonably soon after occupancy.

In addition, the buyer is obligated to maintain the property satisfactorily. Usually, there is a clause in the mortgage under which the buyer agrees to perform proper maintenance, and it is in the buyer's own interest to do this. Some mortgages provide that the holder of the mortgage can have repairs made and add the expense to the mortgage debt if a great deal of deterioration occurs through lack of good maintenance.

Know What You're Signing

It would be to your advantage to have the advice of a qualified real estate attorney before you sign any documents, especially the sales contract. You may also want this attorney to represent you at the closing. Choose an attorney who specializes in the field of real estate. Many good lawyers are not real estate experts and one who is experienced in these matters may save you money and problems in years to come. You will be responsible for paying his fee.

Be sure there is a builder's guarantee and that you know the exact dimensions of your lot. A copy of a recent survey is often provided at the closing. However, you may be responsible for paying for this survey.

Find out what the taxes will be on the property and review the facts about your financial obligation. After purchase, make sure the payments are made promptly each month.

Beware of fraud. Make sure your title of ownership is clear and that there are no liens or claims against the property. It is a good idea to purchase a title insurance policy insuring you against defects in the chain of title.

. . . And Now You're the Owner

Remember, your home is your vehicle for living debt-free. You don't want to do anything that will adversely affect the resale price.

When you become the owner of a used or new home, you agree in your mortgage to keep the property in good condition. This is only common sense. Why sacrifice to buy an expensive house and then allow it to lose value through your neglect? Regularly put aside an amount for annual upkeep allowing for the fact that maintenance costs will vary from year to year.

A house is a complicated mechanism, and you can't expect to know how to keep everything in good working order. If you are handy with tools, you may be able to do some of the repair and improvement work. But don't tamper with expensive equipment and appliances unless you are sure that you know what you're doing. You may void the warranty on such equipment if you attempt to do repairs yourself. When the plumbing, electric, or heating system needs more than minor repairs, it's time to call in an expert.

Money Troubles

If you encounter temporary financial problems that will prevent prompt payment on your mortgage, inform your lender immediately. Don't delay. Often, if your payment record is a good one, an arrangement can be worked out to help you through your difficulties. If your lender will not offer you assistance, contact the nearest HUD field office. It may be able to help.

Don't forget that once the closing has taken place you must continue to make payments according to the terms of the mortgage, no matter what defects you find in the house or who is legally responsible for correcting them.

Real Estate Glossary

abstract
A summary of the history of the legal title to a piece of property.

amortization
Provision for gradually paying off the principal amount of a loan, such as a mortgage loan, at the time of each payment of interest. For example, as each payment toward principal is made, the mortgage amount is reduced or amortized by that amount.

appraisal
An evaluation of the property to determine its value. An appraisal is concerned chiefly with market value—what the house would sell for in the market place.

binder or "offer to purchase"
A receipt for money paid to secure the right to purchase real estate upon agreed terms.

certificate of title
Like a car title, this is the paper that signifies ownership of a house. It usually contains a legal description of the house and its land.

closing costs
Sometimes called settlement costs. Costs in addition to price of the house, including mortgage service charges, title search and insurance, and transfer of ownership charges. Be sure your sales contract clearly states who will pay each of these costs—buyer or seller.

closing day
The date on which the title for property passes from the seller to the buyer and/or the date on which the borrower signs the mortgage.

condominium

Individual ownership of a dwelling unit and an undivided interest in the common areas and facilities which serve the multi-unit project.

cooperative housing or co-op

An apartment building or a group of dwellings owned by residents and operated for their benefit by their elected board of directors. The resident occupies but does not own his unit; rather, he owns a share of stock in the total enterprise.

depreciation

A decline in the value of a house as the result of wear and tear, adverse changes in the neighborhood and its patterns, or for any other reason.

earnest money

The deposit given to the seller by the potential buyer to show that he is serious about buying the house. If the deal goes through, the earnest money is applied against the down payment. If the deal does not go through, it may be forfeited.

easement rights

A right-of-way granted to a person or company authorizing access to go over the owner's land. Electric companies often have easement rights across property.

equity

A buyer's initial and increasing ownership rights in a house as he pays off the mortgage. When the mortgage is fully paid off, the buyer has 100% equity in the house.

escrow funds money

Papers representing financial transactions, which are given to a third party to hold until all conditions in a contract are fulfilled.

hazard insurance

Insurance to protect against damages caused to property by fire, windstorm, and other common hazards.

home mortgage loan

A special kind of long-term loan for buying a house. There are three kinds of mortgage financing for single-family homes in the United States: the conventional mortgage; the VA (Veterans Administration), sometimes called the GI mortgage; and the HUD-insured loan.

HUD approval

There is no such thing as a HUD or FHA-approved house. If a builder advertises "FHA approval" he is misleading you at worst and, at best, stating his belief that his house will meet standards for a HUD-insured mortgage.

mortgage commitment

The written notice from the bank or other lender saying that it will advance you the mortgage funds in a specified amount to enable you to buy the house.

mortgage discount "points"

Discounts (points) are a one-time charge assessed by a lending institution to increase the yield from the mortgage loan to a competitive position with the yield from other types of investments.

mortgage insurance premium

The payment made by a borrower to help defray the cost of mortgage insurance, it is paid to the mortgage insurer, either HUD or a private mortgage insurer. The premium provides a reserve fund to protect lenders against losses on insured mortgage transactions. In the case of a HUD-insured mortgage, the mortgage insurance premium may be a one-time payment when the loan is closed, or it may be collected on a monthly basis.

mortgagee
The bank or lender who loans the money to the mortgagor.

mortgagor
The homeowner who is obligated to repay a mortgage loan on a property he has purchased.

prepaid expenses
The initial deposit at time of closing, for taxes and hazard insurance and the subsequent monthly deposits made to the lender for that purpose.

repair and maintenance
The costs incurred in replacing damaged items or maintaining household systems to prevent damage.

special assessment
A tax for a specific purpose such as providing paved streets or new sewers. People whose properties abut the improved streets or tie into the new sewer must pay the tax.

title
The evidence of a person's legal right to possession of property, normally in the form of a deed.

title company
A company that specializes in insuring title to property.

title insurance
Special insurance which usually protects lenders against loss of their interest in property due to unforeseen occurrences that might be traced to legal flaws in previous ownerships. An owner can protect his interest by purchasing separate coverage.

title search or examination

A check of the title records, generally at the local courthouse, to make sure you are buying the house from the legal owner and that there are no liens, overdue special assessments, or other claims or outstanding restrictive covenants filed in the record.

CHAPTER FIVE

You Gotta Have Wheels . . .

"They ain't givin' you nothin'."
—Ernest Davis

W ill Rogers once observed that America would be the only country in the world to drive to the poor farm in an automobile.

Humor aside, the fact remains that today in most parts of this country it's virtually impossible to get to the poor farm, or anywhere else, without personal transportation.

With the narrow exception of center city residents in major urban areas, a personal vehicle is a necessity for nearly every individual and/or family. Not to mention that many families find it impossible, not merely impractical, to perform daily routines with only one "family car."

With the need for a car a given, the focus shifts to how to incorporate car ownership into the *Live Debt-Free* lifestyle.

This breaks down into three prime considerations:

1. Which vehicle you choose.
2. Where/when you buy it.
3. How you pay for it.

Nobody but you can select the car you really want—or the one you're willing to settle for due to practical (economic) reasons.

Preference in automobiles is a quite personal thing: some demand high performance; others want only basic transportation; some buy with safety in mind. There are as many ideas on the ideal car as there are people.

And this choice—once you have achieved the *Live Debt-Free* way of car buying—is purely yours.

The only car this book is concerned about is the one, or perhaps two, that you will purchase in avoiding forever the Car Payment Monster.

Used Cars

Just as your choice of vehicle is personal, so is whether or not you should consider buying a used car.

It's true, sensational values have been snapped up in the used car market. The three typical best sources for a used car remain:

1. Buying a car you know from someone you know, who takes care of vehicles and who has a legitimate reason for selling. In short, buying once you know the reason the car is being sold and the car's condition.
2. Taking advantage of demographics. If you live in an area loaded with senior citizens, true bargains are available when a driver dies, must stop driving for health reasons, or loses his driver's license.
3. Scanning the paper. Newspaper ads, if read critically, can offer leads. For instance, a salesman had a practically brand new car; he'd transferred to another company which furnished automobiles; his wife liked her car and didn't want his—so a good buy was available.

Let's compare our two car buyers: Luckless Luke, who hasn't read this chapter; and Knowledgeable Kevin, who has.

Luckless Luke, as always, is short of money when his old clunker gasps its last breath. It's gone. He sells it for junk.

Then he sees a newspaper ad blaring, "ONLY $199 down and $199 monthly" for a very basic model. He rushes to the showroom.

Soon he's on wheels again. Complete with a coupon payment book with 60 tickets at $199 each (at 7.5% interest).

For 60 months Luke drives and pays—and by this time his new car has become an old car and he's back on the same treadmill.

For life.

And let's not forget the $12,139 paid for a $9,000 car.

Now shift camera to Knowledgeable Kevin. He has followed the *Live Debt-Free* plan and is, accordingly, now buying his first (used) car for cash.

Once Kevin drives out of the dealership he begins paying $199 monthly—not to any bank or loan company but to his own "auto account."

The difference is that, instead of paying the 7.5% interest, Kevin puts his money in CDs, which will average 8% over the years.

Kevin pays for his next car by withdrawing his $9,000 from his account which now (built by the same $199 monthly that Luke paid) has reached $15,130. (Kevin's "investment" is his willingness to drive one or more used cars he owns outright over the same period. It can be done by pursuing the three avenues we just examined.)

He thus leaves $6,130 sitting in the account which, in another 60 months, has grown to over $9,000—to pay for his next car after 60 months (during which time Knowledgeable Kevin has not put aside one penny for a new car).

After this "free" car he can simply—every other time he buys a car—put aside the equivalent of a car payment.

This way, Kevin buys one new car—and the next is "on the house" via the *Live Debt-Free* system.

As in the section on houses, these figures are used to illustrate a principle: Today more people think in terms of $19,000 cars or $29,000 cars than $9,000 vehicles.

But, again, the principle is exactly the same.

Sell, Don't Trade

Rule one of economical "car trading" is *not* to trade. When the dealer takes your old car in on trade, he juggles figures on both cars to create the illusion you are getting "the buy of a lifetime" (you aren't). In trading in, you're playing the dealer's game.

Anyone familiar with car buying facts of life will assure you that selling your own car then buying "clean" puts you in a much better bargaining position.

How to sell your old car?

Five steps:

1. First find its value. Check the "Blue Book" value (you can check the Kelley Blue Book value of most makes and years on the Web at *www.kbb.com*). Go to used car lots; see what is being asked for models similar to yours. You can also check newspaper ads for comparison.
2. After determining a fair value, cut the price a little to make your car move quickly (still much better than you'd do with a dealer).
3. Advertise. Write an ad listing your car's assets, including price. Work on this ad; rewrite until it's one you couldn't help answering yourself.

4. Answer all questions honestly on the phone when your ad brings response. In fact, use these calls to weed out likely nonbuyers. After a while you'll get the knack of this. (Incidentally, a rule of thumb is that half of the people who say they're coming will actually show up—whether you're selling a car or house or camera.)

5. Accompany the driver on his test drive, encouraging him to drive as long as he wishes. Let him get the "feel" of the car's handling. When he offers you enough cash—and not before—say "yes." It's that simple.

When you have cash or bank check in hand, you're off to the races, looking for the new car.

Car Buying Tips

The sagacity of the fabled Yankee horse trader is legendary. Many of his descendants are around today. A number of these work in auto showrooms. You're up against big leaguers.

Auto dealerships are not charitable institutions; they are businesses. Auto salesmen do not sprout halos above their heads; they are usually genial sorts, likable as all-get-out, extroverts—and far more practiced at wheeling and dealing than you are.

But you can strengthen your hand—unless your faithful jalopy just turned belly up and died—by choosing *when* to buy.

Traditionally, nobody feels like buying a car in depressing February; salesmen are usually way behind on their quotas and, as mentioned elsewhere in this book, it's a great time to venture out.

Also, as imports increasingly threaten the big American automakers, heavy inventories have created more eagerness than usual to accept minimum offers. One dealer has been quoted publicly as saying: "Any offer that's in the black takes a car off this lot."

(By the way, never accept as gospel the "list price" on any vehicle. When car sales begin to s-l-o-w down, the discounts will fly.)

Still another traditional and valid occasion is the end-of-model year. Often you can do even better here, however, if you don't nibble at the first flashy lure. By December, dealers are really anxious to get rid of the previous year's models.

$ 🐃 $

Mention of December brings up another possibility for some—those living near coastal areas with import centers—the end-of-year "dock sales."

We learned about one by a flyer in the mail (although there were extensive newspaper/radio/TV ads). One late December afternoon, the mass sale began.

On January 1, the distributors or dealers would have to pay the annual inventory tax on these trucks (this sale was in vans and pickup trucks only). Therefore, the savings would be "passed along to the buyer."

Actually, there also must have been severe overstock at that moment because this sales effort, at Jacksonville, Florida, was a massive one with band music, free hot dogs and soft drinks, etc. Dozens of salesmen were on hand in the deserted shopping center where the sale was held.

As we entered, a salesman was assigned to us. My wife quipped, "Here's our date for the night—he'll stick with us until we buy or walk out." She was right.

We first explained there would be no trade-in and we would pay cash.

Amid the crowded carnival air our salesman first showed us some expensive, fancy pickups, until we insisted we wanted a sturdy basic truck. He showed us three, identical except in color. We chose white instantly. The window sticker was just under $8,900.

We were ushered to a table with our salesman and the haggling began.

"Look," I kept saying, "I've got $6,000 in the bank and a perfectly good truck parked outside. I just thought that since you people say you are really practically giving these things away, I might take one."

The negotiating process went on for a good two hours—but after our salesman refused to go below $7,000, he called in the sales manager.

The figure finally dropped to $6,500.

Next some kind of regional manager came in. He sadly (almost shedding tears) let the price drop to $6,250.

Somebody new (I don't recall who) entered the interrogation chamber now and that brought the price to $6,150.

Next—and this alone must have taken half an hour—we hammered the price to $6,050.

By this time I was a basket case. Then the "Southeastern Vice President" or some other such deity moved into the Mexican standoff over $6,050 or $6,000. Finally (as the only thing keeping me awake was my wife nodding on my shoulder) we arose in defiance, said "no," and began walking out of the showroom/auditorium.

When we were about 100 feet from our table the Southeastern Deity and a couple of others came running after us, contract and pen in hand.

"Here," the big shot said to the salesman, making a show of peeling $20 bills off a wad, "I'll pay you out of my own pocket the commission you won't make at this price."

There are, I realize, many readers who would not undergo such an exhausting bargaining process for any price. You don't have to.

There are several services that will do the bargaining, in effect, for you. Check with your motor club.

For a small fee (usually $25 or so) these services do a good job of tracking down the best offer available in your area on the car you want.

Some of these services will find a car dealer who will deliver your choice, as you want it, for $100 over dealer cost. Others will get you the fleet sale rate.

Consumer magazines evaluating these services generally give them good ratings. One buyer told how he "went all over" to several dealers, bargained as hard as he could, and still found a car through one of the services at more than $1,000 below the best price he could negotiate.

I have a friend who used perhaps the most ingenious method of all: He faxed his exact specifications for the sports model he wanted to 15 dealers—and the offer he accepted was thousands below the best price available locally.

The System in Action

Earlier we viewed the case histories of Luckless Luke, on a treadmill of paying $199 a month endlessly for minimum cars; and Knowledgeable Kevin, who followed the *Live Debt-Free* plan and had his next car paid for in advance.

So, now, let's see how to quit being Lukes. (In the following examples, our hero doesn't even have to put up with a used car.)

Watch Susie Q. Smarts in action. Her only transportation, a worn-out old station wagon, is driving her crazy with an endless series of $100, $200, and $250 repair bills.

She sells it for $1,000—that's all she has to work with. So:

Her first step: As is the case with Luckless Luke, her only choice is the minimum $9,000 car at $199 down (sales tax, title, tag, etc., will take pretty much the rest of her money) and the advertised "$199 monthly."

But Susie is too smart to get on that endless treadmill wherein car payments are as much a routine of life as brushing your teeth. While Susie pays the $199 down, she arranges her budget so that she can pay off the loan in three years instead of stringing it out for 60 months.

Specifically, instead of paying $199 monthly, she pays a little over half again as much: $309 monthly ($110 more).

In 30 months her car is free and clear. But Susie *keeps paying* the $309 monthly into her bank account marked "car account" for the next 30 months.

Then by the time Luke finally makes his last payment and owns free and clear his 60-month-old car, Susie's "car account" now has approximately $9,500 in it (more than enough to buy for cash the same kind of car as before).

Susie has made the leap from perpetual-payment-making-sucker to debt-free living—all by making a little more effort over the course of 60 months—to benefit *from there on!*

Most people, especially young people, buy cars—often several—before they buy a home.

For many people, this will be the *first bold step* toward living debt-free!

CHAPTER SIX

Don't Let This Happen to You

*"Saving is a very fine thing, especially if
your parents have done it for you."*
—Winston Churchill

L et's read the saga of the Happy Spenders, Hap and Spendy,
a pleasant, attractive young couple. Everybody likes them.
"Going places," people say. Two nice kids, Sis and Junior; Floppy
the dog and Petunia the cat. As our saga opens, Hap has just
been given a promotion down at Salt Mine Inc., where he is a
junior executive.

"Great," exclaimed Spendy. "We can move out of this shoe
box into a home suitable for a growing family."

"Whoopee!" echoed Junior and Sis.

Hap nodded.

The jovial real estate broker, grinning, assured them, "I've
got just what you want." The Happy Spenders, all four, hopped
into the broker's Caddy to zip from "cream puff" to "cream puff"
(at least, the smiling broker called them that) until they finally
found one that really did seem to puff.

"I like it," announced Hap as he looked at the workshop in the garage.

"I love it!" exclaimed Spendy as she stared at a dining room chandelier resembling Liberace's gaudiest light fixture. The ever-so-helpful broker, smiling, worked out some figures on the back of an envelope.

"Put the equity from your old house—won't take long to sell that—on the down payment and closing costs. Your monthly payments will run around $1,200."

Hap hesitated. "Er, isn't there some rule of thumb, about the monthly payment not exceeding weekly income? I get $1,050 a week, but take home only—"

"Shucks," grinned the friendly broker, "nobody takes that stuff seriously any more. After all, you're upwardly mobile. I can get your loan approval right off—got a buddy at the bank." Hap and Spendy looked at each other.

Neglecting the *Live Debt-Free* principles, Hap said, "It will bend the budget. But it's what we want—the man says he can get it for us—what the heck! I look on buying a house as an investment, anyway."

"Sign here"—now the broker's grin was ear to ear—"and leave everything to me."

$ 🪙 $

Four months later, on a beautiful spring day, a happy Hap, puffing slightly, carried Spendy over their mortgaged threshold. Junior and Sis applauded. Floppy barked; Petunia purred. Happiness. But spring was followed by summer, and July was— pardon the language—hot as hell. And August was hell-ier.

$ 🪙 $

"I wish," Spendy sighed, "we'd paid more attention to this

house not being air-conditioned."

"Well," said Hap, "no sense in crying. Or sweating. We'll have to add air conditioning sometime, and it'll never get cheaper, so why not now?"

"We could get a home improvement loan," Spendy nodded.

"Say," Junior spoke up, "add a swimming pool, too—that would really cool us off."

"Oh, Dad, do!" Sis chimed in.

"Honey," Hap turned to Spendy, "the kids have a point. We'd save recreation expenses because we'd stay home more. It would be great for the kids to have their friends over. Come to think of it, Joe Woods was telling me he considers his pool an investment. It adds to the value of his house."

"I heard over the radio," Spendy said, "that you can spread payments over a long time."

"Well," Hap hesitated a moment, "let's do it."

"Whoopee!!!"

The air conditioner purred as gently as Petunia, and the pool was sensational. Spendy and the kids were playing water polo the afternoon that Hap puffed, red-faced, onto the patio.

"Our faithful family jalopy," he announced, "fell apart at Main and Mitzen."

"Get a new car!" Junior shouted.

"Yeah!" said Sis.

"We really should," Spendy said. "With the price of gas what it is now, we would save money by buying a smaller car."

"Maybe," Hap said. "I can look around and find a good used small car."

"Used!" Sis shouted. "What would my friends say?"

"Don't be an old fogy," pleaded Junior.

"I heard," Spendy said, "that Hotshot Motors finances for five years."

Three days later a bright little new brown imported station wagon sparkled in their driveway.

$ 🐷 $

Cometh the mailman, delivering an announcement from old friends Mona and Clyde: "We're coming to visit."

"My!" groaned Spendy. "I'm ashamed for them to see our horrible old living room furniture."

"I'll say," Sis agreed. "Somehow it didn't look so bad in the old house. But here, in the bright sunshine in our big living room, it's horrible."

"Hey," shouted Junior, pulling apart the newspaper as he looked for the comics, "here's a whole section about Wonder Bargain Furniture's 'going out of business' sale." Spendy picked up the ad and read it.

"Yep, it's on the up-and-up. It says, 'Absolutely the last time we will go out of business this year!'"

The three of them persuaded Hap, as soon as he arrived home, to rush to the store. A week later, the new 13-piece living room suite with Distinguished Colonial Styling Crafted by Master Artisans looked truly great in the Happy Spenders' living room.

So great, in fact, that the adjoining dining room set now looked like something belonging on the garbage heap. Luckily, they acted in time for everything still to go on one loan. They wound up refurnishing the entire downstairs. And then because they'd been "such good customers," the nice young salesman offered them the "buy of a lifetime" on a master bedroom suite. Spendy looked at Hap.

"All right," he smiled. "We deserve it, after all these years."

Two weeks later when the washing machine started making funny noises, Spendy didn't even call a repairman. ("Why throw good money after bad?") A new washer—with, of course, a new dryer to match ("Might as well")—took only minutes for the paperwork because "your credit is established." Which turned out to be a real convenience when only two weeks later, the family TV died. And for "just a few dollars more" each month, the enthusiastic salesman pointed out, they "might as well" get automatic color adjusting and surround sound.

"Why not . . . ?"

$ 🎒 $

Life rocked happily along in the neatly furnished, comfortably air-conditioned, luxuriously entertained household of the Happy Spenders. Until spring. In the middle of Big Lake, Hap's outboard motor refused to start. It took him two hours to paddle in, cussing every stroke. But as he paddled, he had an inspiration: "After spending so much on the house, I deserve something for myself for a change." So when he saw a steal of a buy on a new outboard (and by financing it over two years he'd "never miss the payments") the matter was resolved. Hap caught a lot of fish that summer. Ah, the Good Life . . .

$ 🎒 $

Autumn followed summer, then the chill of winter. Hap, in fact, felt especially chilled the first of December when bill-paying time rolled around. He was down to the last few dollars in the checking account when Spendy announced, "The children have to have new winter clothes." Poor Hap winced—but it all turned out to be no problem, no, none at all! The friendly neighborhood bank, just a mile down the road, came through like a trouper with a loan, issuing them another credit card to boot, just "to help with Christmas shopping."

Now whenever cash grew short (and things frequently did

get kind of strained), the Happy Spenders turned to plastic. One weekend, when Spendy paid so much for cut flowers for her club meeting that she didn't have money left for groceries, she remembered that at her supermarket you could charge food on a bank credit card. The plastic got more and more of a workout as hard cash became in ever-shorter supply. It really was heartwarming, Hap thought, the way the friendly firms would tell you, right there on your bill: "At no additional minimum monthly payment, you can charge $340 more."

$ 🐦 $

Then one night, when there was nothing on TV, Hap ran a rough tab of monthly bills on the back of an envelope. Surprising, he thought, how all those "easy" monthly payments added up. But, of course, he could handle it. "I just need a little breathing room." After all, he was bound to get another raise before too long, then everything would be OK. All he needed was a little cash to bridge the gap.

Friendly Finance (such clever ads over the music station) really wanted to help. Getting the loan was so easy, in fact, that the next time things got tight, Hap knew just what to do: he found another loan company that would make him a new loan, even though they already owed Friendly. True, the BYB Company's rates were higher, and lots of charges were made to "set up the account" but he got the money. "Now we can hack it," he told Spendy.

"I'm glad," she said, adding casually, "What does the BYB stand for?"

"Break Your Bones if you don't pay up," Junior piped up.

Hap didn't think that was funny—and the loan did help. So much so that it was months before the Happy Spenders ran completely, totally, absolutely, utterly, out of dollars, dimes, and even pennies. Puzzled, Hap sat down to "tally up." He found every payment coupon book he had—no small task—and got out a pencil and a legal pad. As he picked up each book he wrote down the payment, number of months remaining, and total amount due. He added everything up—and howled! (*See table below.*)

Hap and Spendy's Sad, Sad News

Debt Item	Monthly Payment	Months To Go	Total
Home improvement	346	42	14,532
Car payment	344	33	11,352
Bank loan	232	7	1,624
TV	98	14	1,372
Furniture	248	25	6,200
Washer/dryer	56	22	1,232
Motor	84	13	1,092
Friendly	150	17	2,550
BYB Finance	126	33	4,158
VISA	112	26	2,912
MasterCard	84	26	2,184
Sears	78	25	1,950
Ward's	22	13	286
Total	$1,980		$51,444

Hap looked at the totals as if they were in some strange language. But they were only the beginning. Hap added the monthly payments of $1,980 to the $1,200 house payment for a total monthly payout of $3,180. Then he wrote down his take-home pay of $800 a week, allowing for the fifth paycheck every three months, for an average of $3,467 a month. Next he subtracted $3,180 from $3,467 and found that, after bills were paid, only $287 was left each month for all four Happy Spenders to spend: hardly enough for car fare and lunch money, not to mention groceries and utility bills. Then he remembered these other things.

- The car insurance bill which he hadn't even taken out of the envelope. That would run about $800.
- The bill from the optometrist. Spendy had dropped her glasses, and the new ones, with high fashion frames, had cost $252.
- The vet bill. There was no choice, of course, but to rush Floppy in when that pit bull chewed her up. Floppy wasn't really hurt much, but Hap's wallet was injured a hefty $654.

Hap leaned back in his easy chair with Distinguished Colonial Styling Crafted by Master Artisans as he studied his figures. The words overflowed.

"#*$%@%*!!!"

How to Escape?

As soon as he saw the figures and had recovered, for the moment, from his shock, Hap called Spendy. Now it was her turn to be aghast as she checked the totals of their bills.

Hap then remembered that her figures didn't even include the few other expenses. "Oh, yes, and the car insurance," he said to Spendy. He found the bill, its envelope still unopened, and tore it open: $824. From the desk he also took out the optometrist's bill of $252 and the vet's bill of $654. "Have you made any extra charges on VISA or MasterCard that we haven't gotten the bill for yet?" he asked Spendy.

There were, Spendy remembered, groceries. A time or two. Once it was $202 (she remembered the number because it was almost an even 200). Again for "$120-something." Oh, another time "about $160."

Anything else?

Hap remembered charging some gasoline on his MasterCard, "probably about $50 in all," he guessed.

"Oh," Spendy exclaimed, "that new yellow dress. Only $52—a real bargain. And there was a pair of shoes, $60-something, I think. My new church shoes. Black."

There was the birthday present, Hap remembered, for his mother. "Only $34. Oh-oh! I haven't paid the electric bill yet. That's $200 and something." Hap tried to write down these additional bills on hand, and the ones to come, as best he could guess the amount. "I come up with $2,566 more," he said. "We may have forgotten something, so call it $2,600 at most. We . . ."

"You forgot $300 at least for the quarterly life insurance bill due at the end of this month."

Hap shook his head. "I shouldn't have let that guy talk me into such a big policy."

"But you did. So that means we're almost $3,000 more in debt than even those horrifying figures show."

"Want a drink, honey?" Hap finally asked.

"No," Spendy answered, sweetly. "I want your credit cards."

With all the joy of Lee handing over his sword at Appomattox, Hap took the plastic rectangles from his wallet, and plunked them, one by one, upon the coffee table. Spendy held up a pair of scissors. Hap turned the other way as snip . . . snip . . . snip . . . snip went the scissors. "Next, mine," she said. Snip . . . snip . . . snip. Hap saw in Spendy's eyes a look he had never seen there before; it reminded him of that ethereal stare he'd once seen in a Joan of Arc movie. Spendy took Hap's list of debts off the table and held it up.

"Starting right now, I'm taking full command of our family budget." She studied the list of debts as Hap looked on in awe. "The home improvement loan," she began, "makes our total house payment $1,546 a month. We'll sell the house."

"But, Spendy . . ."

"We'll sell the house."

Hap sighed. "It wouldn't be practical selling the car," she continued, thinking aloud. "We owe about as much as we'd get for it. And we can't afford to be saddled with a junker needing constant repair bills." Hap smiled for the first time since all this began. "The loans," she continued—"there's nothing we can do about them. The bank and Friendly and BYB must be paid in full. Same with VISA and MasterCard and Sears and Ward's." She paused briefly, then went on. "We might as well keep the washer and dryer, since we'd spend that much going to and from laundromats. Besides, I won't have time for a laundromat: I'll soon be working. The TV and the furniture should bring about 10 to 20 cents on the dollar we paid—I mean are paying—for them."

"It can't be that bad. Our nice new . . ."

"Dearest," she said, "the other day, remember, when Chuck Lewis was over here, looking at your outboard motor? I heard him say that if you want to get a bigger one, he'd gladly give you $750 for the old one."

Hap looked away . . .

To be continued.

CHAPTER SEVEN

Credit Cards and All That

"When money talks it often merely says 'goodbye.'"
—Poor Richard Jr.'s Almanac (1906)

Should you, like Hap and Spendy, simply cut all your credit cards in half? It depends. If you simply can't refrain from using the cards impulsively, cutting off all use in this way may be the best idea. More important than any such dramatic gestures, though, is getting a little bit of perspective.

For most consumers, the big question is this: What role should credit cards really play in my financial future? We'll try to find some answers in this chapter.

The problem with credit cards is that we so frequently think of them as something quite different from money; plunking down a card is so much easier to do than taking actual cash from a wallet. Merchants know this well; countless televised sales pitches are based on the idea that a consumer would not spend $29.95 to buy a set of knives if the knives were in front of him in a store and he had only cash to purchase them—but would make that purchase over the telephone using a credit card. There's something impulsive about buying on plastic— and that can be trouble. For many of us, it is just too easy to justify buying things with credit cards.

Then, of course, there's the little problem that your purchases on credit cards can cost you considerably more than the price listed on the item. Remember, with most cards, you're paying interest on the money you're borrowing to make credit card purchases. Lots of interest. I feel the only sane approach is to pay off the entire balance every month and avoid these charges. Unfortunately, after a month or two of carefree charging, this can be quite difficult to do. If you do choose to carry a small amount of debt from month to month, be sure to shop around for the best rate. The interest charges on various cards can differ a great deal; some are as high as 18% yearly!

Best Credit Card Deals

Here are some of the best credit card deals nationally as of this writing, for customers who pay off their monthly balances as well as those who don't. These rates compare with a national average credit card rate of 13.69%. Rates are for conventional credit cards, not premium cards, and information applies to purchases only. Cash advances frequently are charged interest from the date of transaction. Additional fees may be charged—for example, exceeding a credit line, making a payment late, obtaining a cash advance, making an ATM transaction, or having a check returned.

Best Deals for People Who Carry Balances

Rates as of 2003	Annual Fee	Telephone Number
Wachovia Bank		
4.25%[2]	$98	800-922-4684
Pulaski Bank & Trust Co.		
5.50%	$35	800-980-2265
Chase Manhattan Bank USA		
5.90%[1,2]	$0	800-413-5661

Amalgamated Bank of Chicago
7.50%[2] $37   800-723-0303
5 Star Bank
8.50%[2] $35   800-776-2265
Metropolitan National Bank
8.95%[2] $35   800-883-2511
Simmons First National Bank
8.95% $35   800-272-2102
Wachovia Bank
10.24%[2] $0   800-922-4684
State Farm Bank, FSB
11.15%[2] $0   877-SF4-BANK
USAA Savings Bank
11.85%[2] $0   800-365-8722
Roslyn Savings Bank
12.15%[2,3] $0   516-942-6000
Warwick Savings Bank
12.24%[2] $20   845-986-2206
Ballston Spa National Bank
12.96% $0   518-885-6781
AmTrust Bank, Division of Ohio Savings
12.99% $0   888-268-7878
Astoria Federal Savings & Loan Association
12.99% $0   800-ASTORIA
Troy Savings Bank
12.99% $0   518-270-3200
Union Planters Bank
12.99% $0   800-847-7378

[1]No grace period. [2]Variable rate. [3]MasterCard only.

Best Deals for People Who Pay Off
Entire Balance Monthly

Rates as of 2003	Annual Fee	Telephone Number
Chase Manhattan Bank USA		
5.90%[2,3]	$0	800-413-5661
Wachovia Bank		
10.24%[2]	$0	800-922-4684
Amalgamated Bank of Chicago		
10.75%[2,3]	$0	800-723-0303
State Farm Bank, FSB		
11.15%[2]	$0	877-SF4-BANK
5 Star Bank		
11.40%[2]	$0	800-776-2265

Source: Bankrate Inc., North Palm Beach, FL 33408

Credit Card Tip: Some major banks have been quietly offering credit cards with no annual fee on a limited basis to boost business, while keeping customers who are willing to pay an annual fee on the original agreement.

[1]No grace period. [2]Variable rate. [3]MasterCard only.

Credit cards are very convenient; but there is a price for that convenience. If you find that the cards represent too much of a temptation, it may well be appropriate for you to get rid of them. For many consumers, however, a credit card is a useful tool that can be incorporated into a sound financial program— a means of making occasional unexpected purchases within set limits, or a source of emergency funds.

It's not uncommon for a person to have, say, four credit

cards, all charged to the limit, and to be barely able to keep his head above water with the payments. Yet such people are often on the receiving end of notices from other credit card companies informing them that they've been "pre-approved" for yet another card! How, you may ask, can this happen?

Stop and think of the situation from the credit card company's point of view for a moment. The company is not interested in promoting the solvency or stability of its customers—at least, not as long as they can keep on being customers. What the company is interested in is obtaining a huge group of users, people who will turn to the cards regularly and pay high rates of interest for the privilege of doing so. In short, the companies are looking for . . . people who like to use credit cards.

The fact that an individual customer is "charged to the limit" on other cards may not have the negative impact you'd think it would. If you're current with a number of cards, the fact that you use them a great deal makes you more desirable as a customer—not less!

To put it bluntly, credit card companies are always looking for people who like to borrow money. If someone's consumer profile indicates that this is the case, that person's likely to be approached for another card. But the question I would put to you is this: Even if the company thinks you're the kind of person who likes to borrow money—do you agree?

Lending Sources to Avoid

While we're on the subject of the appetites of creditors, it's probably a good idea to review the kinds of money sources you should avoid, no matter what. Much of this book is devoted to showing you ways to establish your financial independence from normal creditors, on the assumption that you're the one who should be in control of your life—and not them. How much more true this principle holds for dealings with the following extremely dangerous creditors!

Never borrow money from . . .

1. An acquaintance or colleague who holds a longstanding grudge against you. It may seem obvious, but such loans are often extended with the unspoken intent of launching a suit to recover the money if you encounter financial difficulty. It may be a genuine olive branch, of course, but then again . . .

2. A pawnbroker. With pawnbrokers, you will pay obscenely high amounts of interest on small loans. What's more, the amount you will be able to borrow will represent only a fraction of your item's actual value. Of course, the broker's business is based on the fact that many of the people he loans money to never return to claim the items they have pawned. Although there is nothing *stopping* you from returning to repay the debt and get your property back, there are much better business environments in which to negotiate if you have to borrow money. (Of course, if you follow the principles outlined in this book, you won't need to borrow in the first place!)

Note: They don't quite fall into the same category as loan sharks, but you are still well advised to stay far away from the "easy terms" consumer lending institutions that offer "consolidation" of your debts—for a price. That price is usually a ridiculously high interest rate. Unless you are in serious financial trouble and are in desperate need of a way to satisfy creditors, you should not be tempted by the televised appeals of these places. (Actually, even those in financial trouble should think twice before signing on with these firms, if only as a result of the nasty reputation held by their legendary collection departments. These boiler rooms are constantly humming, on the prowl for the sizeable portion of the client base who fail to make payments.)

Remember: These organizations exist to make a profit, just like any other business, and that profit comes from you, in the form of hyperinflated interest costs. Decline the invitation.

Best Use of a Credit Card

Earlier we promised to tell about the man who built his house on a VISA card. Sounds silly—until you hear the story. Call him Tim Takecharge, and call his wife Tanya. They had just begun their final year of work before (very early) retirement.

Being followers of the *Live Debt-Free* system, they had paid for their own house long ago; they had also long since paid for the acreage for their retirement home, a heavily forested site overlooking a clear blue lake about 125 miles from their present home. They had also recently sold other investment property, which gave them income for basic living expenses, in effect freeing both their salaries, that final working year, for building their new home.

With Tanya's help, Tim drew his own plans and acted as his own contractor: he got the permits and hired the carpenters, the electricians, the plumbers, the drywall workers, the painters, and so on. To overcome the 125-mile distance, Tim and Tanya would commute every weekend to make arrangements with workers for the work to be done the next week. They took a week's vacation during "drying in" and another during "locking in." But the most interesting part of Tim's project was his financing. He scheduled building so that periods of high material costs were alternated with times of labor intensive (heavy payroll) operations. At each step of construction he would go to building supply stores and charge the needed materials on his VISA while he paid his workers cash. Then he would cut his labor to a minimum so that when his VISA bill came, he could clear his account. He maintained a tightrope balance between paying workers weekly and material costs monthly almost to the end. Only when he pushed, in order to get final inspection, did any balance accrue on his credit card. The house was finished for Christmas dinner and a gala double retirement party on New Year's Day. Then came the final VISA bill—including $40 interest. Imagine financing a house for $40 interest instead of $200,000 or so over decades. Tim and Tanya's story underscores the point that every *Live Debt-Free* reader may want to have a major credit card for convenience. (Try renting a car, for one example, without one.)

CHAPTER EIGHT

Cutting Expenses— Painlessly

"Money is often lost for want of money."
—Thomas Draxe (1616)

In this part of the book, we'll look briefly at a number of simple, painless techniques you can use to reduce day-to-day expenditures . . . and improve your overall financial picture. The ideas range from grocery store bills to health care expenses; taken together, they will show you a number of ways to take control of your financial future.

One woman I know had the bank add on one of those "convenient" credit lines to her bank account—essentially, a credit card stapled onto her checkbook. The temptation became too great; after a while, balancing the checkbook became a thing of the past. Why bother when you "can't bounce a check anymore?" (As long as you keep the credit line under its limit!) One day she stopped long enough to pull out her calculator . . . and realized that, with the balances she had been registering for the past year, she was paying something like 10% *more* in interest charges on every trip to the grocery store!

It was impossible for her to pay off the credit line immediately, but actually the situation was something of a blessing in disguise. In the months it took her to close out the "convenience" she was paying for at such outrageous prices, she decided to compensate by finding ways to cut back on household and other expenses. You can, too—and without depriving yourself! The list that follows is an excellent place to start.

Grocery Bills

Never shop when you're hungry. A recent study showed that grocery bills were an average of 15% higher when compiled by shoppers who had not eaten in the past three to four hours.

Don't buy unnecessary vitamins. Virtually all nutritionists agree that the vast majority of individuals can and should obtain all necessary vitamins and minerals from simply eating a balanced diet. What that means is that unless you are, for instance, a nursing mother or a person with a diagnosed nutritional deficiency, you can safely skip buying vitamins, period. That's something the vitamin industry doesn't like to talk about, but it is true. (In the end, this is probably a personal decision.)

Take SELECTIVE advantage of generic brands. I know, I know. It sounds cheesy. But hear me out. There's a men's clothing store in my area that advertises with the slogan, "There is no status in overpaying." I couldn't agree more; if you don't *get* anything more, there's no sense paying extra. For some supermarket items—usually those you can crowd in the back of your larder where no one can see them—there is simply no excuse for paying for the elusive "brand-name quality." The reason? Some items are *required by law* to be exactly the same in content and composition, regardless of packaging or quantity gimmicks.

Here's a partial list:

Aspirin	Salt
Baking soda	Sugar
Cornstarch	Unbleached flour
Honey	Vinegar
Molasses	Vegetable oil (other than olive oil)
Peanuts	Walnuts
Pecans	

Know what's a bargain when. When it comes to perishable goods, you should be on the lookout for those items that are likely to be in season, plentiful, and priced to sell. Take a look at the following table for some ideas.

Seasonal Buys to Watch For

WINTER (December, January, February)
Apples, broccoli, cranberries, grapefruit, poultry, sweet potatoes, winter squash.

SPRING (March, April, May)
Artichokes, cucumbers, beans, grapefruit, pork, strawberries, turnips.

SUMMER (June, July, August)
Apricots, beets, corn, peaches, pears, peas, plums, radishes, salmon, tomatoes, watermelon.

FALL (September, October, November)
Bananas, cauliflower, chestnuts, parsnips, pumpkins, winter squash.

Household Items, Clothing, Major Purchases

Here's a month-by-month breakdown of other good seasonal buys to watch for. (Remember, of course, that your objective is to find the best *value* for your money, and not necessarily just the lowest price.)

Time Your Purchases

January
Blenders; Christmas ornaments, cards, and wrapping (for next year); coffee makers; irons; lingerie; toasters.

February
Bedding; dishes; drapes; sporting goods; automobiles.

March
Major appliances (dishwashers, refrigerators, and so on).

April
Home entertainment components; skis and other winter sports equipment.

May
Fans and air conditioners; lawn and porch furniture.

June
Automobile tires; home furnishings.

July
Major appliances (dishwashers, refrigerators, and so on).

August
New cars; sporting goods; linen goods.

September
Bicycles; gardening supplies.

October
Home furnishings; men's and boys' clothes.

November
Luggage; toys (compared to December prices).

December
Home entertainment components; nursery items
(blankets, playpens, strollers, and so on).

Health: Your Insurance

These days, more and more companies are offering employees a choice between standard health coverage and a health maintenance organization (HMO). The HMO can be a money-saving option for both the company and the employee, but you should be sure that it is the right choice for you before you make any commitment.

HMOs often cover for free or at minimal costs such care as routine checkups and other common, relatively minor reasons to make a trip to see the doctor. In standard health care arrangements, these are typically out-of-pocket expenses. Prescriptions, too, are likely to cost a great deal less after you sign on with an HMO.

There are disadvantages to joining an HMO, however. You are less likely to develop an ongoing patient relationship with a single doctor, for instance; generally, only physicians who are participating members of the plan will see you. There may be more paperwork involved in out-of-town or emergency care, as well.

Weigh all the pluses and minuses carefully, and then make your choice. You may find that an HMO is right for you!

More Ideas for Saving Money

Want to learn more? You should write for the *Consumer Information Catalog*, detailing hundreds of pamphlets available from the federal government. Here are just a few of the informative titles that have been available:

The Complete Guide to Home Canning
The Consumer's Guide to Long-Term Care Insurance
A Doctor's Advice on Self-Care
Do-It-Yourself Medical Testing (hypertension, pregnancy, etc.)
Facing Surgery? Why Not Get a Second Opinion?
Fish and Seafood Made Easy
Health Care and Finances: A Guide for Adult Children and Their Parents
Growing Vegetables in the Home Garden
Making Bag Lunches, Snacks, and Desserts
Making Meals in Minutes
Myths and Facts of Generic Drugs
Shopping for Food
Thrifty Meals for Two
Why Women Don't Get Mammograms (and Why They Should)
Your Money's Worth in Foods

Send your name and address to:
Consumer Information Catalog
Pueblo, CO 81009

CHAPTER NINE

The Road Back

"Put money in thy pocket."
—William Shakespeare

Hap and Spendy have now seen the elephant and heard the lion. Never again will their lives be the same. When all the figures were first added up—the Moment of Shock—the Happy Spenders' situation seemed hopeless. But by taking drastic action, the now savvy Spenders were able to pull out of debt— tear up the last bill—in only 15 months.

How did they do it? Well, it took some willpower. Here are the steps that helped the intrepid family out of the debt hole.

Spendy . . .

- Got a part-time job with take-home pay of $400 a week.
- Contacted a real estate agent and placed their home on the market. The bank got its money. The most important part of the family credit rating was salvaged.
- Found a three-bedroom rental unit for only $1,000 a month, a savings of $546 a month over their past monthly expenses on shelter.

- Put together a realistic budget based on the techniques described in Chapter One of this book. She was able to set aside a modest amount every month to assuage the various installment debts, the finance companies, and the revolving charge accounts. (At first, she paid the minimum on the cards and installment payments and focused primarily on erasing the finance company loans, with their atrocious interest rates.) She estimated the entire process would take the family 18 months; after that, they would be free and clear and could think about owning their own home again.

Hap . . .

- Got his friend Chuck to take over payments on the outboard motor. (It was a great deal for Chuck!)
- Did a little moonlighting to make the budget crunch easier. (But he didn't overextend himself and threaten his primary job!)
- Orchestrated a massive garage sale that netted nearly $600 one weekend. (It went straight into the family bank account.)

Sis . . .

- Took a 10-hour-a-week job at a local department store. (It was more fun that she thought it would be; she was on the same shift as her friend Jane from school.)

Junior . . .

- Took a paper route and passed along the proceeds. (Every little bit counts!)

With everyone kicking in, and by cutting every possible corner, the family beat their deadline by three months. On the night the last installment debt was paid off, they took the opportunity to celebrate together; a "special dinner" had been promised. Everyone sat down as Mom unveiled . . .

Buy-one-get-one-free hot dogs with generic mustard on day-old rolls. There was even some flat root beer to pass around.

"Just kidding," she said, smiling. "How long has it been since we went out to dinner, anyway?"

$ 🐷 $

A few months later they were ahead of their budget and ready to resume normal living. They did this, of course, with a crash program. Crash programming is, in fact, just about the only way that any family or individual can get out of heavy debt in a bearable amount of time without resorting to bankruptcy. Suppose Family X discovers it has amassed debts equal to two years' income—twice as bad as the Spenders. Or that it is Family Y, three years behind (yes, it happens). In these cases crash programming will take longer. The exact time will, of course, depend on individual circumstances, but it is the only way out besides bankruptcy.

If you do opt for bankruptcy, you'll need a good lawyer, not me. When it's all over, pick up the next chapter and go on to happier days from there.

$ 🐷 $

Credit counselors, dealing with hundreds of cases of crash programming out of debt, have come up with several ways to help. Some agencies, for example, contact all creditors, establish a temporary moratorium, and set up a plan wherein the debtors' entire income, except for a living allowance, is paid to the counseling agency, which prorates the money to creditors on a set schedule. Public agencies of this kind are excellent. Warning: They are not to be confused with private groups calling themselves by similar names, who do the same thing for a high fee (which makes the debtors owe even more).

However, many people, like the savvy Spenders, crash program all on their own. Books have been written on this alone, and more will be; but for all practical purposes the basic tenets of swift personal economic recovery are:

1. Face reality.
2. Make a plan of action.
3. Implement the plan.

What Such Plans of Action Require

1. *Increasing income.* For example, from one paycheck to two (as Hap and Spendy did). Of course, Hap's moonlighting helped too. The kids' self-motivated employment was extremely helpful psychologically, even if the dollar amount wasn't great. In families that already have two paychecks, the one most capable of earning more by moonlighting might take two jobs during the crash program, the other doing more on the home front to take up the slack.

2. *Reducing expenditures.* Become money conscious; shop carefully; buy only what's absolutely necessary; remember the old-fashioned "make do."

3. *Getting enough slack in the line* so that everybody can live with the plan—and so that some unexpected expense doesn't sabotage the Good Ship Recovery.

Being reasonable is the key. Don't walk five miles to work through snow and ice; replace your Caddy with an economy car. Don't expect to feed a family on peanut butter and canned tuna; become an expert at "101 Ways to Fix Economy Meals"— yes, they can be delicious. Don't glumly stay at home on weekends; a hiking, swimming, and picnic visit to a state or federal park costs peanuts but can be a very rewarding, relaxing experience. Furthermore, if you think you can reach debt-free heaven in 18 months, figure on 20; it's encouraging to get ahead but demoralizing to fall behind schedule if something unexpected happens.

Question and Answer

Q: In theory, reading about somebody else's life, a crash program seems easy. But, in real life—if you are doing it—isn't it demoralizing, discouraging?

A: On the contrary, a crash program can be an inspiring time, even one of the most fully alive times of one's life. Many people live more intensely during the heat of economic battle; every paycheck makes an advance and sets the enemy back. Week by week, month by month, they push closer to the goal.

Often, people who have crash programmed, looking back at what others would consider a period of hardship, recall their struggle—not just their victory—as one of the most truly satisfying times of their lives.

CHAPTER TEN

Only Fools Retire—Smart People Restart!

"Whoever has money sails in a fair wind."
—*Petronius (circa* 60 A.D.)

Surely you've heard it too: "Never retire—you'll work yourself to death! I wish I were only working a forty-hour week again, with two-day weekends and holidays and vacations and all that good stuff!" Why do people say things like that? I think it's because the people who do say this are doing *what they want to do,* and it's awfully easy to lose track of time in such a happy situation.

Retirement . . . the word has changed dramatically since the last century. The social security pension originated with Germany's iron chancellor, Otto von Bismarck, who was really interested in guns, not butter. When pressured by public opinion to make some concessions toward social progress, he devised what seemed like an idealistic, almost Utopian program, called the old-age pension. It was the first one. And, golly, was it generous! At age 65 the worker would no longer have to toddle to the factory or shop; he could rock on his own front porch and a check, believe it or not, would arrive every month. Happy days were here, thought the populace! Of course, von Bismarck still spent about 95 cents for guns for every nickel allotted for butter, because at that time all of 2% of the population lived past age 65.

Since politicians are almost never original thinkers, practically every nation in the world seized upon age 65 as the time for "retirement." When FDR became president in the throes of the Great Depression and the American Social Security System was born, the program was debated in detail and every nuance questioned. But virtually no thought was given to the age that retirement would begin. That was already settled at 65; everybody knew that! But fate was to play a few tricks on the politicians. For one thing, people started living longer. And some began retiring at 62, not 65, despite reduced benefits. It just took a little planning, foresight, and economic management. Then another factor entered. Many major American companies, whose executives had been enjoying four-martini lunches while the Japanese were working like crazy, found sales going d-o-w-n. Got to cut costs, reasoned the top executives, presumably during a six-martini catered lobster lunch in the penthouse. "Look at our payroll," shouted some genius in a three-piece suit. "That's where all our money goes! Let's get rid of those darn workers!"

And so early retirement was born, a curse to the unprepared but a gift from heaven to the foresighted—including, of course, you. People who would normally have had to wait until 65 to retire were able to "escape" as much as a decade earlier. New doors open . . .

$ 🐷 $

To talk about retirement, we should first talk about work. What is the most important thing in life? How about doing the work that makes you spring eagerly out of bed each morning to rush to that day's exciting adventures? Right! Almost all of us, deep within, know what is right for us, what we really want to do. Unfortunately, few of us can earn our living that way. Those who do are called "lucky." But maybe they're more clever than lucky; maybe they know something that we don't. If so, we could learn from them. I'll bet that the majority of such people have accepted—and the point of this chapter is to help you, too, to accept—two unpopular premises.

- *Unpopular but true premise #1:* The jobs that are the most rewarding to do usually pay the least (and vice versa).
- *Unpopular but true premise #2:* The more desirable an area as a place to live, the harder it is to make a living there.

With this in mind, let's redefine our goal:

- To do what we want to,
- Where we want to do it,
- And make a living at it (and plan for retirement)!

Consider a few examples.

- An artist who turns out illustrations for an ad agency with imagination and flair makes good money. Yet she wants to be a serious artist, and traveling that route could mean years of uncertain or nonexistent income. If only she had the money to make the change.
- An architect dreams of designing energy-efficient homes using passive solar energy but is stuck on a job where all plans, by company policy, must be conventional. He could go on his own—if only he had the money.

- A newspaper reporter, a mere cog in the news machinery of a big-city newspaper, yearns to go to a wilderness area, similar to the place she grew up, buy and edit a weekly newspaper, and become a part of the community. She could easily edit and publish a weekly—if only she had the money to buy it.
- A county agent is inwardly tired of walking the rows of other people's corn. He wants to live by the soil himself—if only he had the money to start.

Such examples are endless.

$ 🐷 $

Let's stop the clock a moment. Let's quit talking about other people's dreams and think of your own. On these next few lines, write down what you are doing now.

_____

_____

_____

_____

_____

Now what you really, deep down inside want to do—for now and the rest of your life.

_____

_____

_____

_____

_____

Now go one step further than we have in our other examples. This concerns you. Let's project how much money it would take to make your dream come true. Figure high. Making a major move almost always takes more money than foreseen. In your enthusiasm at the thought of being able to do what you've always dreamed of doing, solid judgment sometimes gets a bit mushy.

Do you want to buy a business? If so, figure your down payment; then add what it will cost you to survive the first year. Count on no income the first year. Whatever you get will put you ahead for year two.

Want to go freelance—words or art or photos? Again, figure how long it should be before you're self-supporting, bank the money to last you those years, then double the number of years you had estimated. When leaving slavery for the promised land, you want to make sure you stay there once you get there.

Write down your estimate of what you need for your plan.

Goal: $_____

Now, assuming you have figured high, add another 20%, just to be sure. The figure thus becomes:

Goal: $_____

This figure may shock you. But so may others to come. Since your mortgage is paid, why not consider making payments every month, putting your money *in* the bank instead of paying it *to* the bank. Only don't call these "mortgage payments" but "freedom payments." Suppose you had been paying $1,000 principal and interest on your mortgage. Once you own your own home, you invest this in conservative but relatively high-yielding avenues such as income-producing utilities stocks, and Ginnie Mae mutual funds. You should do better in practice, but take 10% as your average yield. In 10 years you will have accumulated more than $200,000. Is that enough to buy your dream? It should buy lots of dreams. For one thing, if left at rest at the same 10% interest, it would bring you a nest egg of $20,000 each year without touching principal. What a subsidy to start your own show!

This figure of $20,000 assumes you pay the taxes on your interest each year, in keeping with a rising income. But suppose you can set aside the nonmortgage payment only? No problem. Simply use part of the annual income to defray the taxes on the income. The first year, for example, your investment would total $12,673, and you'd pay income tax on $673 in interest. In the 28% tax bracket, this comes to $188. Of course, you've already paid withholding taxes on the $12,000, since that is after-tax, "take-home" pay.

No matter what your income bracket is, the figures remain impressive. If your payment is only $500 a month, you still accumulate, paying the taxes annually, more than $100,000. Lots of people have had their dreams come true on lots less than that.

Once the income issue is settled, two major questions remain in retirement: where and what? Each of these decisions will not only affect your health and happiness after you stop working but, indeed, could help determine how long you live to enjoy retirement. Studies show conclusively that people with secure financial means live longer than those who must live with inadequate or uncertain income. Carrying this evidence a little further, it follows that people who live where they want to live will also live longer. Someone who hates cold weather does not want to spend his or her golden years in North Dakota. Talk things over with your partner, probe deeply, work together. With planning, you can see to it that the "declining years" are instead the "ascending years." You have a lot to look forward to!

CHAPTER ELEVEN

The Beauty of the Individual Retirement Account

"With money you are a dragon, without it a worm."
—Chinese proverb

We have said before and we repeat: This book will not try to tell you what to do with your money once you are out of debt. That's your business. But if you want to retain a bit of the money you acquire, then follow the rule: Invest—don't speculate.

$ 🐷 $

In speculating, the point is to multiply money in minutes (at the race track) or days/weeks (commodity market, stock options). Few do so consistently. In investing, you relax and allow your wealth to accumulate slowly instead of quickly. With a little patience, you *can* get rich this way.

Take, for one example, your Individual Retirement Account (IRA). For many it's still a tax-sheltered investment, and a very good one. With the IRA's principle of relatively small deposits, currently $3,000 a year maximum, over a long number of years, it is the surest path to financial security. Three thousand a year is $250 each month. Start at, say, age 22. Since IRAs are long term, they pay higher interest than many investments; estimate a 10% to 10.5% return over a period of decades. To get a rough idea of how this builds—remember, looking so far into the future is only an educated guess—follow the banker's "rule of 72." Divide the interest rate into 72 for the number of years to determine how long your savings will take to double. In this way you can estimate that:

- In seven years (age 29) your first month's deposit has doubled (to $500).
- In 14 years (age 36) that initial deposit is worth $1,000.
- In 21 years (age 43) this one deposit has grown to $2,000.
- In 28 years (age 50) it has doubled again to $4,000.
- By 35 years (age 57) it's $8,000.
- By 42 years at age 64—still before traditional retirement at 65—that initial $250 deposit has turned over and turned over until it's worth $16,000.

In fact, if someone had started an IRA at 22 and made only a single payment of $250, he or she would still have $17,500 at the age of retirement. And if you put in $250 a month starting at age 22, by age 64 you could take out $16,000 each and every month and not run out of money until you were 106 years old.

$ 🐷 $

This has not been an exercise in arithmetic slipped in to annoy people who don't like math. It's purely to demonstrate that the slow, over-the-years route is the way to safely and securely amass a considerable sum of money. It's also to point out another consideration. If a mere IRA will bring such potential returns for so small a monthly sum invested month after month, year after year, is there much point in trying to save more money "for old age"?

Question and Answer

Q: Interest rates fluctuate widely. Certificates of deposit, for example, went from 14% and even 16% down to 6% and 7% within a decade. Won't this throw out all your figures on old age security?

A: Not at all. Interest rates have always fluctuated and always will. You might make a wild guess that your IRA on retirement will be worth $1,700,000, and instead it will turn out to be worth only $1,200,000, or soar upward to $2,200,000. Either way, you aren't exactly standing at the end of a Salvation Army soup line. Chances are strong that, since interest rates and inflation travel pretty much together over the long haul, the issue will be moot.

CHAPTER TWELVE

"Give a Little . . . Gain a Lot!"

"Economy is the art of making the most of life."
—*Maxims for Revolutionists* (1903)

"Nobody rides on both ends of the line." This French proverb is the key to this whole book. Give a little. When you're ready to buy your $200,000 (or whatever) home, don't rush to sign the mortgage papers. Instead, move into the smaller house/condominium for about five years while making the same payment you will make on your permanent home; then you move into your permanent home and live there happily ever after, or as long as you like. But after five more years of the same payments, you have paid off the mortgage of your permanent home.

You make mortgage payments for 10 years—and you quit. Hereafter, so long as you live, you will be mortgage-free. And mortgage-free is, of course, the key to debt-free. You can take the $2,000 or so that you would have been paying the bankers every month for 20 more years and spend it for your benefit instead of theirs. Or you might decide to put it in the bank. After 20 years you have accumulated a tidy little nest egg. To be specific, your monthly $2,000 would, at 10% interest, have multiplied to over $1,530,000. If you have used part of your interest earnings to defray income tax on interest accumulated, you would have less—but still enough money to do what you wanted to do, within reason, the rest of your life.

However, this isn't quite the whole story. We've been "talking money." Now let's talk fun. Enjoying life. Enriching your existence. You may never have thought of it, but people who have traveled that route can tell you that following the *Live Debt-Free* formula can be as enjoyable as it is practical. Young or middle-young couples who have taken the two-step way to a permanent home often find that the years in the temporary first house turn out to be some of the happiest of their lives. A log cabin on a lake, for example. Sure, commuting is bad (although not half as bad when you can do it together), but the home environment contrasts crowded workaday streets. Or a loft condominium in a fishing village, sun coming in through the skylight under which a struggling artist once painted. Or a small town-house downtown offering a glimpse of mid-city life that will be long remembered. Sure, the place is too small for keeps—but for just five years . . .

Readers have recognized by now that the main thrust of this book is to contradict the long-prevailing illusion that "being out of debt means you have everything paid for except, of course, your house." This is indeed an illusion because escaping mortgage payments in 10 years instead of 30 will not merely save you a staggering sum of money, it's the key to taking control of your life. Money opens many doors otherwise closed, and "money makes money." Simply follow the map I have given you to crash-program out of debt, then take off from there.

This book isn't really about credit or money or economics. *Live Debt-Free* means really living life to its fullest: living the life you want. Happy living!

The Price Is Right . . . Somewhere

"Money is not good except it be spread."
Francis Bacon

Many people decide to take an aggressive approach to improving their financial picture: They move somewhere cheaper to live!

Cost-of-living problems among residents of the larger metropolitan areas are nothing new. Residents of New York City are expected to "get used to" paying $10 for a movie ticket and $150 for a parking fine. (Let's not even discuss how much a night out at a good restaurant will run you in Manhattan.)

Now let's examine the relative expense levels of 20 promising, almost forgotten American cities. These urban areas may not be the glitziest places you've ever visited, but they do offer the affordable, quality living environments that may be just what you're looking for. Changing your surroundings by relocating to one of these areas may make your financial picture a good deal brighter.

Since much of this book focuses on inventive techniques for you to consider in purchasing a home, I have highlighted cities that seem to present particularly attractive real estate prices. Please note that, in some cities, a low cost of living is accompanied by a local economy facing challenges that constrict the job market. Of course, if your objective is primarily to isolate a good real estate market, such a city may well be worth looking at closely.

Should you move? Only you can answer that. Obviously, a lot will depend on the job prospects in your field in a given geographical area. If you're looking for livable cities to prospect in, however—cities where you may be better off financially with a comparable job—start with this list.

(All figures are based on prevailing prices at time of research for this book. These figures will change over time.)

Amarillo, Texas

Location: In northwestern part of Texas, approximately
60 miles from the New Mexico border.

Other nearby cities: Dallas, Texas (358 miles); Albuquerque,
New Mexico (290 miles).

Television stations: Four network affiliates, one public broadcasting affiliate.

Estimated population: 170,000.

Write: Amarillo Chamber of Commerce, 1000 South Polk
Street, Amarillo, TX 79105.

The Bottom Line

Overall, costs in the Amarillo area rank 8%–10% lower than
the national average. Housing (a category that combines mortgage and rental units) and utilities costs are each over 10%
lower than the average.

In Amarillo, you will pay . . .

- $55 for electricity.
- $1,516 for auto insurance (based on the average for a
  single male age 27).

Brownsville, Texas

Location: On southern tip of Texas on Rio Grande.

Other nearby cities: Corpus Christi, Texas (approximately 120 miles); Laredo, Texas (approximately 140 miles).

Television stations: Three network affiliates, one public broadcasting affiliate.

Estimated population: 139,000.

Write: Brownsville Chamber of Commerce, 1600 East Elizabeth Street, Brownsville, TX 78520.

The Bottom Line

Overall, costs in Brownsville rank approximately 10% lower than the national average. Housing (a category that combines rental and mortgage units) is a whopping 20% lower than the average.

In Brownsville/Harlingen, you will pay . . .

- $48 for electricity.
- $1,639 for auto insurance (based on the average for a single male age 27).
- $53 for a routine dental cleaning and exam (adult).
- $112,400 for an average home.
- 8.25% sales tax (state and local).
- $.75 for a one-way commuter fare.

Canton, Ohio

Location: In northeastern part of Ohio, approximately 75 miles inland from Lake Erie.

Other nearby cities: Pittsburgh, Pennsylvania (approximately 60 miles); Cleveland, Ohio (approximately 90 miles).

Television stations: One independent station.

Estimated population: 81,000.

Write: Canton Regional Chamber of Commerce, 222 Market Avenue, North, Canton, OH 44702.

The Bottom Line

Overall, costs in the Canton area rank 4% lower than the national average. Housing (a category that combines both rental and mortgage units) is approximately 16% below the average.

In Canton, you will pay . . .

- $74 for electricity.
- $1,570 for auto insurance (based on the average for a single male age 27).
- $58 for a routine dental cleaning and exam (adult).
- $161,500 for an average home.
- 5.75% sales tax (state and local).
- $1.00 for a one-way commuter fare.

Colorado Springs, Colorado

Location: Central Colorado.

Other nearby cities: Denver, Colorado (approximately 80 miles); Pueblo, Colorado (approximately 40 miles).

Television stations: Four network affiliates, one public broadcasting affiliate.

Estimated population: 360,800.

Write: Colorado Springs Chamber of Commerce, 2 North Cascade, Suite 110, Colorado Springs, CO 80903.

The Bottom Line
Overall, costs in the Colorado Springs metropolitan area rank 4% lower than the national average. Utilities cost nearly 30% less than average here.

In Colorado Springs, you will pay . . .

- $46 for electricity.
- $2,226 for auto insurance (based on the average for a single male age 27).
- $62 for a routine dental cleaning and exam (adult).
- $156,200 for an average home.
- 6.1% sales tax (state and local).
- $1.25 for a one-way commuter fare.

Columbus, Georgia

Location: In western part of Georgia, on the Chattahoochee River.

Other nearby cities: Atlanta, Georgia (approximately 80 miles).

Television stations: Four network affiliates, one public broadcasting affiliate.

Estimated population: 200,000.

Write: Greater Columbus Chamber of Commerce, 1200 Sixth Avenue, Columbus, GA 31902.

The Bottom Line

Overall, costs in the Columbus area rank 17% lower than the national average.

In Columbus, you will pay . . .

- $55 for electricity.
- $1,516 for auto insurance (based on the average for a single male age 27).
- $58 for a routine dental cleaning and exam (adult).
- $124,700 for an average home.
- 7% sales tax (state and local).
- $1.00 for a one-way commuter fare.

Decatur, Illinois

Location: Central Illinois.

Other nearby cities: Indianapolis, Indiana (approximately 180 miles); St. Louis, Missouri (approximately 150 miles).

Television stations: Two network affiliates, one independent.

Estimated population: 82,000.

Write: Chamber of Commerce, 243 South Water Street, Suite 100, Decatur, IL 62523.

The Bottom Line
Overall, costs in the Decatur area rank 16% lower than the national average.

In Decatur, you will pay . . .

- $59 for electricity.
- $1,614 for auto insurance (based on the average for a single male age 27).
- $57 for a routine dental cleaning and exam (adult).
- $82,600 for an average home.
- 7.5% sales tax (state and local).
- $.75 for a one-way commuter fare.

Fort Wayne, Indiana

Location: In northeastern part of Indiana, at junction of Maumee and St. Joseph Rivers.

Other nearby cities: Indianapolis, Indiana (118 miles); Toledo, Ohio (101 miles).

Television stations: Four network affiliates, one public broadcasting affiliate.

Estimated population: 205,700.

Write: Greater Fort Wayne Chamber of Commerce, 826 Ewing Street, Fort Wayne, IN 46802.

The Bottom Line

Overall, costs in the Fort Wayne area rank 22% lower than the national average. Housing (a category that combines rental and mortgage units) is 15% lower than the national average.

In Fort Wayne, you will pay . . .

- $50 for electricity.
- $1,354 for auto insurance (based on the average for a single male age 27).
- $55 for a routine dental cleaning and exam (adult).
- $96,900 for an average home.
- 5% sales tax (state and local).
- $1.00 for a one-way commuter fare.

Green Bay, Wisconsin

Location: In eastern part of Wisconsin, at mouth of Green Bay.

Other nearby cities: Milwaukee, Wisconsin (approximately 100 miles).

Television stations: Four network affiliates, one public broadcasting affiliate, one independent.

Estimated population: 102,000.

Write: Green Bay Area Chamber of Commerce, P.O. Box 1660, Green Bay, WI 54305.

The Bottom Line

Overall, costs in the Green Bay area rank 5% lower than the national average. Utility expenses are 12% lower than the average.

In Green Bay, you will pay . . .

- $47 for electricity.
- $1,406 for auto insurance (based on the average for a single male age 27).
- $59 for a routine dental cleaning and exam (adult).
- $132,000 for an average home.
- 5% sales tax (state and local).
- $1.00 for a one-way commuter fare.

Kansas City, Missouri

Location: In western part of Missouri, at junction of Missouri and Kansas Rivers.

Other nearby cities: Omaha, Nebraska (201 miles); St. Louis, Missouri (257 miles).

Television stations: Four network affiliates, one public broadcasting affiliate, one independent.

Estimated population: 441,500.

Write: The Greater Kansas City Chamber of Commerce, 2600 Commerce Tower, 911 Main Street, Kansas City, MO 64105.

The Bottom Line
Overall, costs in the Kansas City metropolitan area rank 11% lower than the national average.

In Kansas City, you will pay . . .

- $55 for electricity.
- $2,022 for auto insurance (based on the average for a single male age 27).
- $58 for a routine dental cleaning and exam (adult).
- $122,700 for an average home.
- 6.41% sales tax (state and local).
- $1.00 for a one-way commuter fare.

Louisville, Kentucky

Location: In north central part of Kentucky, on the Ohio River.

Other nearby cities: Cincinnati, Ohio (101 miles).

Television stations: Four network affiliates, two public broadcasting affiliates, one independent.

Estimated population: 256,000.

Write: Greater Louisville Inc. Chamber of Commerce, 614 West Main Street, Suite 6000, Louisville, KY 40202.

The Bottom Line

Overall, costs in the Louisville area rank 11% lower than the national average. Housing (a category that combines rental and mortgage units) is 10% lower than the average; utilities are 3% lower.

In Louisville, you will pay . . .

- $41 for electricity.
- $1,850 for auto insurance (based on the average for a single male age 27).
- $57 for a routine dental cleaning and exam (adult).
- $140,600 for an average home.
- 6% sales tax (state and local).
- $1.00 for a one-way commuter fare.

Lubbock, Texas

Location: In northwestern part of Texas, approximately 60 miles from the New Mexico border.

Other nearby cities: Dallas, Texas (approximately 240 miles).

Television stations: Four network affiliates, one public broadcasting affiliate.

Estimated population: 199,500.

Write: Lubbock Chamber of Commerce, 1301 Broadway Street, Suite 101, Lubbock, TX 79401.

The Bottom Line

Overall, costs in the Lubbock metropolitan area rank 14% lower than the national average. Grocery items are a particularly good value here, with prices estimated at 15% below the national average.

In Lubbock, you will pay . . .

- $42 for electricity.
- $1,531 for auto insurance (based on the average for a single male age 27).
- $54 for a routine dental cleaning and exam (adult).
- $91,100 for an average home.
- 7.88% sales tax (state and local).
- $1.00 for a one-way commuter fare.

Mobile, Alabama

Location: In southern part of Alabama, on Mobile Bay.

Other nearby cities: New Orleans, Louisiana (approximately 150 miles); Pensacola, Florida (approximately 60 miles).

Television stations: Three network affiliates, one public broadcasting affiliate.

Estimated population: 199,000.

Write: Mobile Area Chamber of Commerce, 451 Government Street, Mobile, AL 36602.

The Bottom Line
Overall, costs in the Mobile area rank 15% lower than the national average.

In Mobile, you will pay . . .

- $51 for electricity.
- $1,370 for auto insurance (based on the average for a single male age 27).
- $57 for a routine dental cleaning and exam (adult).
- $91,300 for an average home.
- 9% sales tax (state and local).
- Free electric trolley transportation downtown.

Oklahoma City, Oklahoma

Location: Central Oklahoma.

Other nearby cities: Tulsa, Oklahoma (approximately 130 miles).

Television stations: Four network affiliates, one public broadcasting affiliate.

Estimated population: 506,000.

Write: Greater Oklahoma City Chamber of Commerce, 123 Park Avenue, Oklahoma City, OK 73102.

The Bottom Line

Overall, costs in the Oklahoma City area rank 13% lower than the national average.

In Oklahoma City, you will pay . . .

- $49 for electricity.
- $1,506 for auto insurance (based on the average for a single male age 27).
- $54 for a routine dental cleaning and exam (adult).
- $114,000 for an average home.
- 7.38% sales tax (state and local).
- $1.10 for a one-way commuter fare.

Omaha, Nebraska

Location: In eastern part of Nebraska, on the Missouri River.

Other nearby cities: Kansas City, Missouri (approximately 200 miles); Des Moines, Iowa (approximately 140 miles).

Television stations: Four network affiliates, one public broadcasting affiliate, one independent.

Estimated population: 390,000.

Write: Greater Omaha Chamber of Commerce, 1301 Harney Street, Omaha, NE 68102.

The Bottom Line

Overall, costs in the Omaha area rank 13% lower than the national average. Housing costs (a category that combines mortgage and rental units) are 18% lower than the average; grocery items are 8% lower.

In Omaha, you will pay . . .

- $49 for electricity.
- $1,902 for auto insurance (based on the average for a single male age 27).
- $55 for a routine dental cleaning and exam (adult).
- $121,700 for an average home.
- 6.5% sales tax (state and local).
- $1.25 for a one-way commuter fare.

Salt Lake City, Utah

Location: In northern part of Utah, on the Great Salt Lake.

Other nearby cities: Las Vegas, Nevada (433 miles); Denver, Colorado (504 miles).

Television stations: Four network affiliates, one public broadcasting affiliate, one independent.

Estimated population: 181,700.

Write: Chamber of Commerce, 175 East 400 South, Suite 600, Salt Lake City, UT 84111.

The Bottom Line
Overall, costs in the Salt Lake City area rank 5% lower than the national average.

In Salt Lake City, you will pay . . .

- $43 for electricity.
- $940 for auto insurance (based on the average for a single male age 27).
- $58 for a routine dental cleaning and exam (adult).
- $160,000 for an average home.
- 6.13% sales tax (state and local).
- $1.25 for a one-way commuter fare.

Tulsa, Oklahoma

Location: In northwestern part of Oklahoma, on the Arkansas River.

Other nearby cities: Oklahoma City, Oklahoma (approximately 130 miles); Wichita, Kansas (approximately 200 miles).

Television stations: Four network affiliates, one public broadcasting affiliate.

Estimated population: 393,000.

Write: Tulsa Metro Chamber of Commerce, 616 South Boston Avenue, Tulsa, OK 74119.

The Bottom Line

Overall, costs in the Tulsa area rank 13% lower than the national average. Housing (a category that combines rental and mortgage units) is 13% lower than the average; utilities are 11% lower.

In Tulsa, you will pay . . .

- $39 for electricity.
- $1,552 for auto insurance (based on the average for a single male age 27).
- $56 for a routine dental cleaning and exam (adult).
- $130,180 for an average home.
- 7.5% sales tax (state and local).
- $1.00 for a one-way commuter fare.

Waco, Texas

Location: In western central part of Texas, on the Brazos River.

Other nearby cities: Dallas, Texas (approximately 140 miles).

Television stations: Three network affiliates, one public broadcasting affiliate.

Estimated population: 113,700.

Write: Greater Waco Chamber of Commerce, 101 South University Parks Drive, Waco, TX 76701.

The Bottom Line

Overall, costs in the Waco area rank 16% lower than the national average. Housing (a category that combines rental and mortgage units) is 20% lower than the average.

In Waco, you will pay . . .

- $53 for electricity.
- $1,585 for auto insurance (based on the average for a single male age 27).
- $55 for a routine dental cleaning and exam (adult).
- $91,650 for an average home.
- 8.25% sales tax (state and local).
- $1.00 for a one-way commuter fare.

Waterloo, Iowa

Location: In northeastern part of Iowa.

Other nearby cities: Des Moines, Iowa (approximately 120 miles); Milwaukee, Wisconsin (approximately 290 miles).

Television stations: Three network affiliates.

Estimated population: 68,750.

Write: Waterloo Chamber of Commerce, P.O. Box 1587, Waterloo, IA 50704.

The Bottom Line

Overall, costs in the Waterloo area rank 12% lower than the national average. Housing (a category that combines rental and mortgage units) is 6% lower than the average.

In Waterloo, you will pay . . .

- $62 for electricity.
- $1,090 for auto insurance (based on the average for a single male age 27).
- $65 for a routine dental cleaning and exam (adult).
- $145,270 for an average home.
- 6% sales tax (state and local).
- $1.50 for a one-way commuter fare.

Wichita, Kansas

Location: In southeastern part of Kansas, on the Arkansas River.

Other nearby cities: Kansas City, Missouri (approximately 200 miles).

Television stations: Three network affiliates, one independent.

Estimated population: 344,000.

Write: Wichita Area Chamber of Commerce, 350 West Douglas, Wichita, KS 67202.

The Bottom Line
Overall, costs in the Wichita area rank 2% lower than the national average.

In Wichita, you will pay . . .

- $59 for electricity.
- $1,580 for auto insurance (based on the average for a single male age 27).
- $56 for a routine dental cleaning and exam (adult).
- $141,900 for an average home.
- 5.9% sales tax (state and local).
- $1.00 for a one-way commuter fare.

Youngstown, Ohio

Location: In northeastern part of Ohio, near the Pennsylvania border.

Other nearby cities: Cleveland, Ohio (approximately 50 miles).

Television stations: Four network affiliates, one public broad-casting affiliate.

Estimated population: 82,000.

Write: Chamber of Commerce, 1200 Stambaugh Building, Youngstown, OH 44503.

The Bottom Line

Overall, costs in the Youngstown area rank 6% lower than the national average. Housing (a category that combines rental and mortgage units) is 18% below the average.

In Youngstown, you will pay . . .

- $74 for electricity.
- $1,452 for auto insurance (based on the average for a single male age 27).
- $58 for a routine dental cleaning and exam (adult).
- $131,000 for an average home.
- 6% sales tax (state and local).
- $1.00 for a one-way commuter fare.

Index

About the Author

TED CARROLL was a prize-winning newspaper editor noted for a light touch on heavy topics, especially economics. His editorials were widely reprinted in major newspapers, including the *Christian Science Monitor*, in magazines and in diverse publications ranging from the newsletters of Wall Street brokerage firms to a plumbers' union house organ. They have been condensed in the *Conservative Digest*, *Reader's Digest*, and other publications. His commentary on the economic scene spanned 23 years as editor of the Bradenton, Florida *Herald*; editorial page editor of the Delaware County, Pennsylvania *Daily Times*; and associate editor, editorial page, *The Florida Times-Union*. He was an internationally published writer of fiction with a novel and 144 short stories in print. Until his death in 1998, he lived with his wife, Virginia Carroll, in Ormond Beach, Florida.